SECOND EDITION

TOP NOTCH

English for Today's World

2A

WITH WORKBOOK

Joan Saslow • Allen Ascher

With *Top Notch Pop Songs and Karaoke*
by Rob Morsberger

PEARSON
Longman

Top Notch: English for Today's World 2A with Workbook, Second Edition

Pearson Education, 10 Bank Street, White Plains, NY 10606

Staff credits: The people who made up the *Top Notch 2* team—representing editorial, design, production, and manufacturing—are Rhea Banker, Peter Benson, Elizabeth Carlson, Diane Cipollone, Aerin Csigay, Dave Dickey, Warren Fischbach, Shelley Gazes, Aliza Greenblatt, Ray Keating, and Mike Kemper.

Cover design: Rhea Banker
Cover photo: Sprint/Corbis
Text design: Elizabeth Carlson and Wendy Wolf
Text composition: Quarasan!
Text font: 9/10 Stone Sans, ITC Stone Sans

Library of Congress Cataloging-in-Publication Data

Saslow, Joan M.
Top notch: English for today's world / Joan Saslow, Allen Ascher; with Top Notch pop songs and Karaoke by Rob Morsberger. — 2nd ed.
p. cm.
ISBN 0-13-246988-X (set) — ISBN 0-13-247038-1 (v. 1) — ISBN 0-13-247048-9 (v. 2) — ISBN 0-13-247027-6 (v. 3) 1. English language — Textbooks for foreign speakers. 2. English language — Problems, exercises, etc. I. Ascher, Allen. II. Title.
PE1128.S2757 2011
428.2'4 — dc22
2010019162

ISBN 13: 978-0-13-247050-6
ISBN 10: 0-13-247050-0

Photo credits: All original photography by Sharon Hoogstraten and David Mager. Page 2 (background) Shutterstock.com, (top left) Will & Deni McIntyre/Getty Images, (top middle left) Blend RF/Glow Images, (top middle right) Michael Goldman/Masterfile, (top right) Jeff Greenberg/PhotoEdit Inc., (bottom left) Michael Newman/PhotoEdit Inc., (bottom middle left) Dorling Kindersley; p. 5 Shutterstock.com; p. 7 (Egypt) Dallas & John Heaton/Corbis, (Mexico) John Neubauer/PhotoEdit Inc., (China) Picture Finders Ltd./eStock Photo, (Peru) Fotolia.com, (Japan) Dallas & John Heaton/Corbis, (Rio) Mathias Oppersdorff/Photo Researchers, Inc., (Feijoada) Fotolia.com; p. 8 (middle) Shutterstock.com, (bottom) Shutterstock.com; p. 10 (middle) Shutterstock.com, (1) Shutterstock.com, (2) Shutterstock.com, (3) Shutterstock.com; p. 11 Sunstar/Photo Researchers, Inc.; p. 12 (1) Fotolia.com, (2) Steve Vidler/eStock Photo, (3) Superstock, (4) Rafael Macia/Photo Researchers, Inc.; p. 14 (left) Warner Bros/Photofest, (middle left) Photofest, (middle right) DreamWorks/Photofest, (right) Paramount Pictures/Photofest; p. 16 Stephane Cardinale/People Avenue/Corbis; p. 18 (action) Original Films/Bob Marshak/The Kobal Collection, (horror) Warner Bros/The Kobal Collection, (sci-fi) MGM/The Kobal Collection, (animated) Globe Photos, (comedy) Morgan Creek/The Kobal Collection, (drama) Paramount/The Kobal Collection, (documentary) Les Gibbon/Alamy, (musical) Simon Fergusson/Getty Images; p. 20 Shutterstock.com; p. 21 (top left) Shutterstock.com, (top right) Shutterstock.com, (bottom left) Shutterstock.com, (bottom right) Shutterstock.com; p. 22 Shutterstock.com; p. 23 Miramax Films/Photofest; p. 26 (top right logos) Shutterstock.com, (single) Jeff Greenberg/PhotoEdit Inc., (double) Jeff Greenberg/PhotoEdit Inc.; p. 28 Shutterstock.com; p. 30 Shutterstock.com, (top right) Inspirestock RF/Getty Images; p. 32 (towels) Comstock.com, (hangers) Murat Sentürk/Fotolia, (iron) Michael Matisse/Getty Images, (dryer) Getty Images, (make up) Jeff Greenberg/Index Stock Imagery, (turn down) Comstock.com, (bring up) David Bartruff Inc.; p. 33 Shutterstock.com; p. 34 (left) Dorling Kindersley, (middle) Rudy Van Briel/PhotoEdit Inc., (right) Look Die Bildagentur Fotografen Gmbtt/Alamy; p. 37 (left) Shutterstock.com, (right) Shutterstock.com; p. 38 (left) Shutterstock.com, (sedan) Courtesy DaimlerChrysler Corporation, (compact) Shutterstock.com, (wagon) Dorling Kindersley, (van) Oleksiy Maksymenko/Alamy, (convertible) Motoring Picture Library/Alamy, (SUV) Kurt Wittman/Corbis, (sports) Adam Woolfitt/Corbis, (luxury) Ron Kimball Photography; p. 44 (bottom right) Shutterstock.com;p. 45 (Lexor) Photolibrary.com, (Sea) Ron Kimball Photography; (Outing) Izmostock/Alamy, (Invocation) Photolibrary.com, (Turbo) Photolibrary.com, (Micro) Dreamstime.com, (Amigo) Shutterstock.com, (Overland) Izmostock/Alamy; p. 46 iStockphoto.com; p. 47 Shutterstock.com; p. 50 (top left) Shutterstock.com, (top middle) Shutterstock.com, (top right) Shutterstock.com, (bottom left) Shutterstock.com, (bottom middle) Photolibrary.com, (bottom right) Shutterstock.com; p. 52 (2) Shutterstock.com, (4) Aina Zimnika/Fotolia, (6) Shutterstock.com, (7) Shutterstock.com, (8) Shutterstock.com, (10) Shutterstock.com, (12) Shutterstock.com, (13) Shutterstock.com, (14) Shutterstock.com, (15) Shutterstock.com, (16) Shutterstock.com, p. 56 (left) Shutterstock.com, (right) Michael Bermant, MD, Board Certified, American Board of Plastic Surgery, www.plasticsurgery4u.com; p. 57 Bill Losh/Getty Images; p. 58 (left) Shutterstock.com, (right) Shutterstock.com; p. 59 (1) Shutterstock.com, (2) Shutterstock.com, (3) Shutterstock.com, (4) Shutterstock.com; p. W1 (top left) Will & Deni McIntyre/Getty Images, (top middle left) Michael Goldman/Masterfile, (top middle right) P. Sheandell/age fotostock, (top right) Jeff Greenberg/PhotoEdit Inc.; p. W4 Angelo Cavalli/Index Stock Imagery; p. W7 Shutterstock.com; p. W14 Shutterstock.com; p. W18 Shutterstock.com; p. W22 Shutterstock.com; p. W24 Fredde Lieberman; p. W32 Shutterstock.com; p. W39 Shutterstock.com; p. W45 Shutterstock.com; p. W49 Shutterstock.com; p. W50 Getty Images; p. W51 Shutterstock.com.

Illustration credits: Steve Attoe, p. 6, W5 (top), W21, W46; Sue Carlson, p. 35; John Ceballos, pp. 25, 37, 49; Mark Collins, pp. 27, 42 (left), W17; Leanne Franson, pp. W3, W5 (bottom), W29; John Hovell, p. 9; Brian Hughes, pp. 24 (bottom), 41, W30, W37; Stephen Hutchings, p. W20; Adam Larkum, p. 61; Pat Lewis, p. 10; Suzanne Morgenstern, pp. W18, W19, W48; Andy Myer, pp. 16 (left, center), W10; Dusan Petricic, pp. 8, 33, 41, W25, W33; Jake Rickwood, p. 24 (top); Neil Stewart, p. W42; Anna Veltfort, pp. 16 (right), 29, 42 (right), W38; Jean Wisenbaugh, p. 13.

Text credits: Page 46 (article) Teens Health.org, (c) 2007–2009, Adapted with permission.

Printed in the United States of America
10 11 12—V082—17 16 15 14 13

CONTENTS

Learning Objectives for 2A and 2B iv

To the Teacher viii

About Your *ActiveBook* Self-Study Disc ix

UNIT 1 Greetings and Small Talk 2

UNIT 2 Movies and Entertainment 14

UNIT 3 Staying in Hotels 26

UNIT 4 Cars and Driving 38

UNIT 5 Personal Care and Appearance 50

Grammar Booster 122

Writing Booster 139

Top Notch Pop Lyrics 149

WORKBOOK

UNIT 1 .... W1

UNIT 2 .... W9

UNIT 3 .... W17

UNIT 4 .... W27

UNIT 5 .... W36

About the Authors .... last page

Learning Objectives

Unit	Communication Goals	Vocabulary	Grammar
1 **Greetings and Small Talk** page 2	• Get reacquainted with someone • Greet a visitor to your country • Discuss gestures and customs • Describe an interesting experience	• Tourist activities • Participial adjectives to describe experiences	• The present perfect ◦ Statements and yes / no questions ◦ Form and usage ◦ Past participles of irregular verbs ◦ With already, yet, ever, and before ◦ Common errors **GRAMMAR BOOSTER** • The present perfect ◦ Past participles: regular and irregular ◦ Questions with What or Which ◦ Yet and already: expansion ◦ Ever, never, and before ◦ Common errors
2 **Movies and Entertainment** page 14	• Apologize for being late • Discuss preferences for movie genres • Describe and recommend movies • Discuss effects of movie violence on viewers	• Explanations for being late • Movie genres • Phrases to describe preferences • Adjectives to describe movies	• The present perfect ◦ With for and since ◦ Other uses • Would rather + base form ◦ Form and usage ◦ Statements, questions, and answers ◦ Common errors **GRAMMAR BOOSTER** • The present perfect continuous • The present participle: spelling • Expressing preferences: review
3 **Staying in Hotels** page 26	• Check into a hotel • Leave and take a telephone message • Request hotel housekeeping services • Choose hotels and explain reasons for choices	• Hotel room types and features • Hotel services • Hotel room amenities and services	• Had better ◦ Usage ◦ Vs. should ◦ Contractions • The future with will ◦ Form and usage ◦ Contractions **GRAMMAR BOOSTER** • Obligation: have to / must • Suggestions and advice: could / should / ought to / had better • Expectation: be supposed to • Will: other uses; vs. be going to
4 **Cars and Driving** page 38	• Describe a car accident • Report a problem with a car • Rent a car • Discuss good and bad driving	• Car types • Car parts • Ways to show concern • Causes of car accidents • Phrasal verbs for talking about cars • Aggressive driving behavior	• The past continuous ◦ Form and usage ◦ Vs. the simple past tense • Direct objects with phrasal verbs **GRAMMAR BOOSTER** • The past continuous: other uses • Nouns and pronouns: review
5 **Personal Care and Appearance** page 50	• Ask for something in a store • Request salon services • Discuss ways to improve one's appearance • Define and discuss the meaning of beauty	• Salon services • Personal care products • Ways to discuss beauty	• Indefinite quantities and amounts ◦ Some and any ◦ A lot of, many, and much • Indefinite pronouns: someone / no one / anyone **GRAMMAR BOOSTER** • Some and any: indefiniteness • Too many, too much, and enough • Indefinite pronouns: something, anything, and nothing

Conversation Strategies	Listening/ Pronunciation	Reading	Writing
• Use "I don't think so." to soften a negative answer • Say "I know!" to exclaim that you've discovered an answer • Use "Welcome to ___." to greet someone to a new place • Say "That's great." to acknowledge someone's positive experience	**Listening Skills:** • Listen to associate • Listen for details **Pronunciation:** • Sound reduction in the present perfect	**Texts:** • A poster about customs • A magazine article about non-verbal communication • A geographical map • A photo story **Skills/Strategies:** • Identify supporting details • Personalize information	**Task:** • Write a description of a fascinating, strange, thrilling, or frightening experience **WRITING BOOSTER** • Avoiding run-on sentences
• Apologize and provide a reason when late • Say "That's fine." to reassure • Offer to repay someone with "How much do I owe?" • Use "What would you say to ___?" to propose an idea • Soften a negative response with "To tell you the truth, . . ."	**Listening Skills:** • Listen for main ideas • Listen to infer meaning • Dictation **Pronunciation:** • Reduction of h	**Texts:** • A movie website • Movie reviews • A textbook excerpt about violence in movies • A photo story **Skills/Strategies:** • Confirm content • Evaluate ideas	**Task:** • Write an essay about violence in movies and on TV **WRITING BOOSTER** • Paragraphs • Topic sentences
• Say "Let's see." to indicate you're checking information • Make a formal, polite request with "May I ___?" • Say "Here you go." when handing someone something • Use "By the way, . . ." to introduce new information • Say "Would you like to leave a message?" if someone isn't available	**Listening Skills:** • Listen to take phone messages • Listen for main ideas • Listen for details **Pronunciation:** • Contractions with will	**Texts:** • A hotel website • Phone message slips • A hotel guide book • A city map • A photo story **Skills/Strategies:** • Draw conclusions • Identify supporting details • Interpret a map	**Task:** • Write a paragraph explaining the reasons for choosing a hotel **WRITING BOOSTER** • Avoiding sentence fragments with because or since
• Express concern about another's condition after an accident • Express relief when hearing all is OK • Use "only" to minimize the seriousness of a situation • Use "actually" to soften negative information • Empathize with "I'm sorry to hear that."	**Listening Skills:** • Listen to summarize • Listen to infer outcomes • Listen for main ideas **Pronunciation:** • Stress of particles in phrasal verbs	**Texts:** • A rental car brochure • Rental car case studies • A feature article about defensive driving • A driving behavior survey • A photo story **Skills/Strategies:** • Understand from context • Critical thinking	**Task:** • Write a paragraph comparing good and bad drivers **WRITING BOOSTER** • Connecting words and sentences: and, in addition, furthermore, and therefore
• Use "Excuse me." to initiate a conversation with a salesperson • Confirm information by repeating it with rising intonation • Use "Not at all." to show you don't mind an inconvenience	**Listening Skills:** • Listen to summarize • Listen to take notes **Pronunciation:** • Pronunciation of unstressed vowels	**Texts:** • A hotel spa advertisement • A health advice column • A photo story **Skills/Strategies:** • Predict • Confirm content • Apply information	**Task:** • Write a letter on how to improve appearance **WRITING BOOSTER** • Writing a formal letter

Unit	Communication Goals	Vocabulary	Grammar
6 **Eating Well** page 62	• Talk about food passions • Make an excuse to decline food • Discuss lifestyle changes you have made • Describe local dishes	• Nutrition terminology • Food passions • Excuses for not eating something • Food descriptions	• Use to / used to • Negative yes / no questions • Offers and suggestions with Why don't . . . ? **GRAMMAR BOOSTER** • Use to / used to: expansion ◦ Be used to vs. get used to ◦ Would + base form • More about negative yes / no questions; Why don't . . . ?
7 **About Personality** page 74	• Get to know someone's likes and dislikes • Cheer someone up • Discuss personality and its origin • Examine the impact of birth order on personality	• Positive and negative adjectives • Terms to discuss psychology and personality	• Gerunds and infinitives as direct objects • Gerunds as objects of prepositions **GRAMMAR BOOSTER** • Gerunds and infinitives: other functions • Negative gerunds
8 **The Arts** page 86	• Recommend a museum • Ask about and describe art objects • Talk about artistic talent and where it comes from • Discuss your favorite artists and the reasons you like them	• Kinds of art • Positive adjectives • Materials and objects • Describing how art affects us	• The passive voice ◦ Form, meaning, and usage ◦ Statements and questions **GRAMMAR BOOSTER** • Transitive and intransitive verbs • The passive voice: form in all tenses
9 **Living with Computers** page 98	• Troubleshoot computer problems • Recommend a better deal • Describe how you use computers • Discuss the social impact of the Internet	• Computer parts • Ways to reassure someone • Computer terms and commands • Internet activities	• The infinitive of purpose • Comparisons with as . . . as ◦ Meaning and usage ◦ Just, almost, quite, nearly **GRAMMAR BOOSTER** • Expressing purpose with in order to and for • As . . . as to compare adverbs • Comparatives / superlatives: review
10 **Ethics and Values** page 110	• Discuss ethical choices • Return someone else's property • Express personal values • Discuss acts of kindness and honesty	• Ways to confirm a response • Ethical choices • Ways to acknowledge thanks • Personal values	• The real and unreal conditional ◦ Form, usage, common errors • Possessive pronouns / Whose ◦ Form, usage, common errors **GRAMMAR BOOSTER** • Present and future factual conditionals: usage and common errors • Order of clauses: punctuation • Possessive nouns: review and expansion • Pronouns: summary

Grammar Booster .... **page 122**
Writing Booster .... **page 139**
***Top Notch Pop* Lyrics** .... **page 149**
ActiveBook Self-Study Disc .... **Inside back cover**

Conversation Strategies	Listening/ Pronunciation	Reading	Writing
• Provide an emphatic affirmative response with "Definitely." • Offer food with "Please help yourself." • Acknowledge someone's efforts by saying something positive • Soften the rejection of an offer with "I'll pass on the ___." • Use a negative question to express surprise • Use "It's not a problem." to downplay inconvenience	**Listening Skills:** • Listen for details • Listen to personalize **Pronunciation:** • Sound reduction: use to / used to	**Texts:** • A healthy eating pyramid • Descriptions of types of diets • A magazine article about eating habits • A lifestyle survey • Menu ingredients • A photo story **Skills/Strategies:** • Understand from context • Summarize • Compare and contrast	**Task:** • Write a persuasive paragraph about the differences in present-day and past diets *WRITING BOOSTER* • Connecting ideas: subordinating conjunctions
• Clarify an earlier question with "Well, for example, ..." • Buy time to think with "Let's see." • Use auxiliary do to emphasize a verb • Thank someone for showing interest • Offer empathy with "I know what you mean."	**Listening Skills:** • Listen for main ideas • Listen for specific information • Synthesize information • Infer information **Pronunciation:** • Reduction of to in infinitives	**Texts:** • A pop psychology website • A textbook excerpt about the nature / nurture controversy • Personality surveys • A photo story **Skills/Strategies:** • Support reasoning with details • Understand from context • Make personal comparisons	**Task:** • Write an essay describing someone's personality *WRITING BOOSTER* • Parallel structure
• Say "Be sure not to miss ___." to emphasize the importance of an action • Introduce the first aspect of an opinion with "For one thing, ..." • Express enthusiasm for what someone has said with "No kidding!" • Invite someone's opinion with "What do you think of ___?"	**Listening Skills:** • Understand from context • Listen to take notes • Infer point of view **Pronunciation:** • Emphatic stress	**Texts:** • Museum descriptions • A book excerpt about the origin of artistic talent • An artistic survey • A photo story **Skills/Strategies:** • Recognize the main idea • Identify supporting details • Paraphrase	**Task:** • Write a detailed description of a decorative object *WRITING BOOSTER* • Providing supporting details
• Ask for assistance with "Could you take a look at ___?" • Introduce an explanation with "Well, ..." • Make a suggestion with "Why don't you try ___ing?" • Express interest informally with "Oh, yeah?" • Use "Everyone says ..." to introduce a popular opinion • Say "Well, I've heard ___." to support a point of view	**Listening Skills:** • Infer meaning • Listen for the main idea • Listen for details **Pronunciation:** • Stress in as ... as phrases	**Texts:** • A computer troubleshooting website • A computer user survey • Newspaper clippings about the Internet • A photo story **Skills/Strategies:** • Understand from context • Relate to personal experience	**Task:** • Write an essay evaluating the benefits and problems of the Internet *WRITING BOOSTER* • Organizing ideas
• Say "You think so?" to reconfirm someone's opinion • Provide an emphatic affirmative response with "Absolutely." • Acknowledge thanks with "Don't mention it."	**Listening Skills:** • Listen to infer information • Listen for main ideas • Understand vocabulary from context • Listen to apply new vocabulary • Support reasoning with details **Pronunciation:** • Assimilation of d + y in would you	**Texts:** • A personal values self-test • Print and online news stories about kindness and honesty • A photo story **Skills/Strategies:** • Predict • Infer meaning • Summarize • Interpret information • Relate to personal experience	**Task:** • Write an essay about someone's personal choice *WRITING BOOSTER* • Introducing conflicting ideas

To the Teacher

What is *Top Notch?*

Top Notch is a six-level* communicative course that prepares adults and young adults to interact successfully and confidently with both native and non-native speakers of English.

The goal of the *Top Notch* course is to make English unforgettable through:

- Multiple exposures to new language
- Numerous opportunities to practice it
- Deliberate and intensive recycling

The *Top Notch* course has two beginning levels: *Top Notch* Fundamentals for true beginners and *Top Notch* 1 for false beginners.

Each full level of *Top Notch* contains enough material for 60 to 90 hours of classroom instruction. A wide choice of supplementary components makes it easy to tailor *Top Notch* to the needs of your classes.

**Summit* 1 and *Summit* 2 are the titles of the fifth and sixth levels of the *Top Notch* course. All Student's Books are available in split editions with bound-in workbooks.

The *Top Notch* instructional design

Daily confirmation of progress

Each easy-to-follow two-page lesson begins with a clearly stated communication goal. All lesson activities are integrated with the goal and systematically build toward a final speaking activity in which students demonstrate achievement of the goal. "Can-do" statements in each unit ensure students' awareness of the continuum of their progress.

A purposeful conversation syllabus

Memorable conversation models provide essential and practical social language that students can carry "in their pockets" for use in real life. Guided conversation pair work enables students to modify, personalize, and extend each model so they can use it to communicate their <u>own</u> thoughts and needs. Free discussion activities are carefully crafted so students can continually retrieve and use the language from the models. All conversation models are informed by the Longman Corpus of Spoken American English.

An emphasis on cultural fluency

Recognizing that English is a global language, *Top Notch* actively equips students to interact socially with people from a variety of cultures and deliberately prepares them to understand accented speakers from diverse language backgrounds.

Intensive vocabulary development

Students actively work with a rich vocabulary of high-frequency words, collocations, and expressions in all units of the Student's Book. Clear illustrations and definitions clarify meaning and provide support for independent study, review, and test preparation. Systematic recycling promotes smooth and continued acquisition of vocabulary from the beginning to the advanced levels of the course.

A dynamic approach to grammar

An explicit grammar syllabus is supported by charts containing clear grammar rules, relevant examples, and explanations of meaning and use. Numerous grammar exercises provide focused practice, and grammar usage is continually activated in communication exercises that illustrate the grammar being learned.

A dedicated pronunciation syllabus

Focused pronunciation, rhythm, and intonation practice is included in each unit, providing application of each pronunciation point to the target language of the unit and facilitating comprehensible pronunciation.

ActiveBook

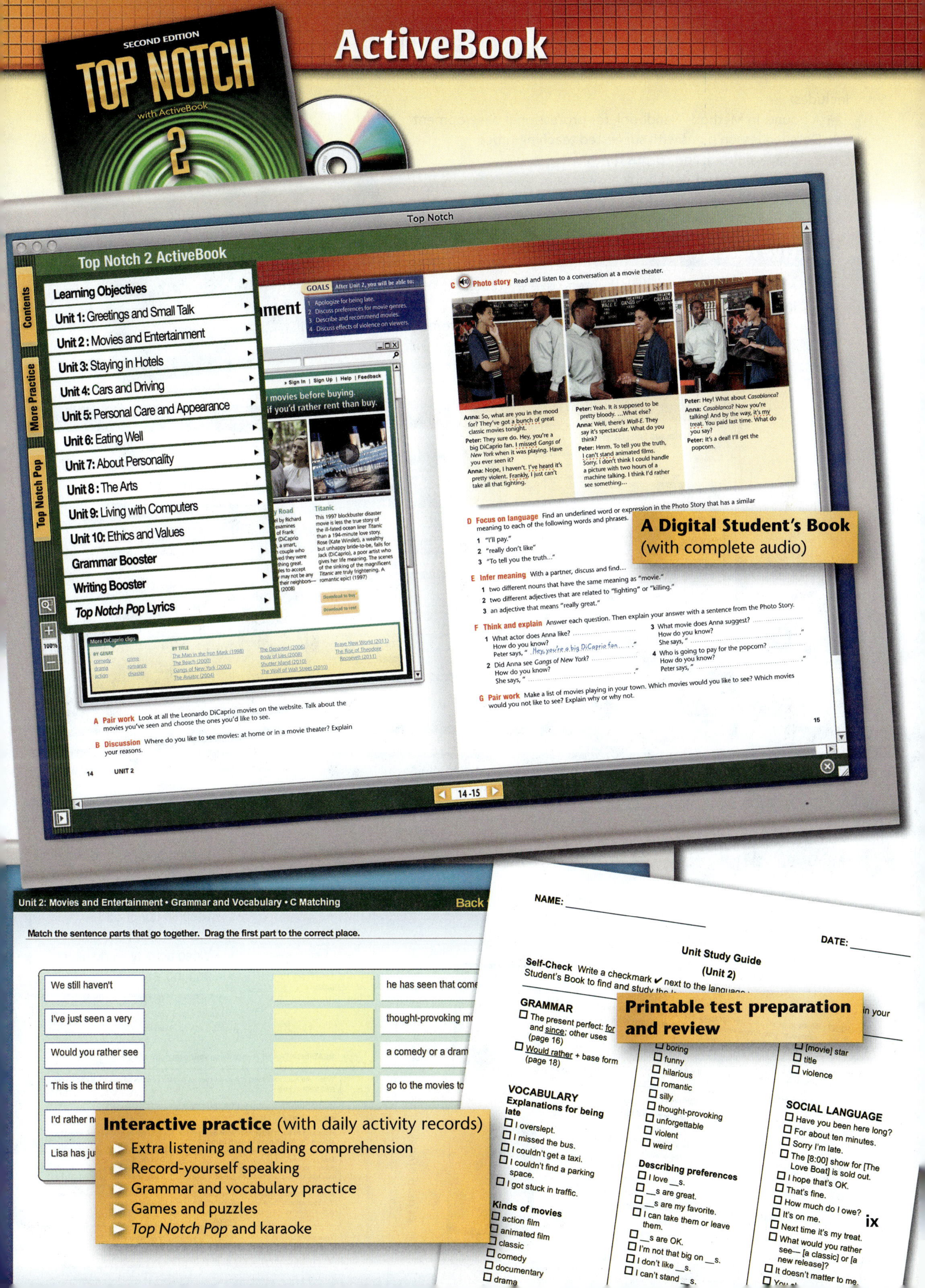
A Digital Student's Book
(with complete audio)
Printable test preparation and review
Interactive practice (with daily activity records)
Extra listening and reading comprehension
Record-yourself speaking
Grammar and vocabulary practice
Games and puzzles
Top Notch Pop and karaoke

The Teacher's Edition and Lesson Planner

Includes:

- A bound-in Methods Handbook for professional development
- Detailed lesson plans with suggested teaching times
- Language, culture, and corpus notes
- Student's Book and Workbook answer keys
- Audioscripts
- *Top Notch TV* teaching notes
- **ActiveTeach**
  - A Digital Student's Book with interactive whiteboard (IWB) software
  - Instantly accessible audio and *Top Notch TV* video
  - Interactive exercises from the Student's *ActiveBook* for in-class use
  - A complete menu of printable extension activities

The Digital Student's Book

With zoom, write, highlight, save and other IWB tools.

Top Notch TV

A hilarious situation comedy, authentic unrehearsed on-the-street interviews, and *Top Notch Pop* karaoke.

Printable Extension Activities

Including:

- Writing process worksheets
- Vocabulary flashcards
- Learning strategies
- Graphic organizers
- Pronunciation activities
- Video activity worksheets

and more . . .

Page 1 of 2

NAME: ____________ DATE: ____________

Writing Process Worksheet
(Accompanies Unit 7, page 84)

ASSIGNMENT: Write at least two paragraphs about the personality of someone you know well. Use vocabulary and ideas from Lessons 3 and 4.

1. PREWRITING

A. Think of a person you know well. Complete the following survey about that person.

Introvert or Extrovert?

Extroverts tend to:	Introverts tend to:
❍ enjoy being in a group.	❍ enjoy being alone.
❍ need to interact with others.	❍ avoid interacting unnecessarily.
❍ be active.	❍ be quiet.
❍ be interested in events.	❍ be interested in feelings.
❍ talk without thinking.	❍ think without talking.
❍ be easy to understand.	❍ be hard to understand.
❍ know many people a little.	❍ know few people, but well.
❍ talk.	❍ listen.
❍ seek excitement.	❍ seek peace.
❍ express their opinions openly.	❍ keep their ideas to themselves.
Total extrovert selections: ______	**Total introvert selections:** ______

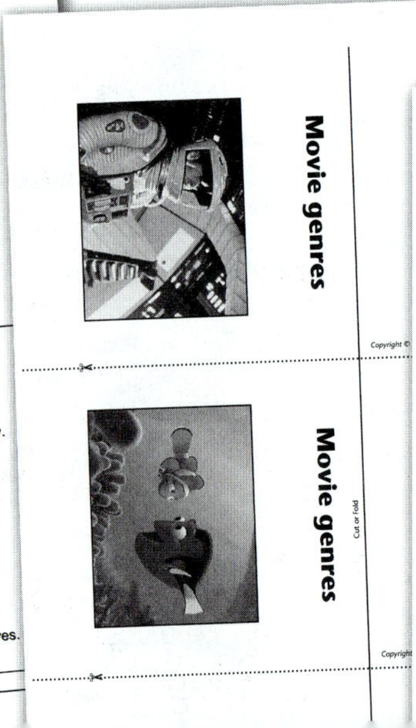

NAME: ____________

Learning Strategy
(Unit 5, page 56, Reading)

READING STRATEGY: clarifying your own point of view

When you read something that expresses an opinion or gives advice, think about your own point of view.

PRACTICE

Respond to each letter with your own advice. Do you agree or disagree with the advice Dr. Weiss gave to each person?

Dear Dr. Weiss:
When I was young, I was a chocoholic. I ate a lot of chocolate, but never gained any weight. Now that I'm older, I can't eat anything without gaining weight! I've heard that liposuction is the answer to an overweight person's dreams. What's up with that?
Dawson

Your advice:

Dear Dr. Weiss:
I'm a 24-year-old man who is already losing his hair! Dr. Weiss, I'm looking for a wife and I'm afraid no woman will want to marry a 25-year-old baldie! I need some advice.
Calvin

Your advice:

Other components

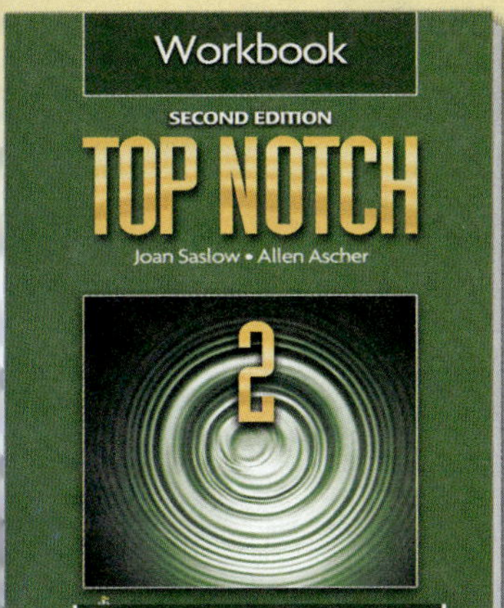

Workbook

Daily assignments that reinforce each lesson.

Classroom Audio Program

Includes a variety of authentic regional and non-native accents.

Complete Assessment Package

Ready-made achievement tests. Software provides option to edit, delete, or add items.

Full-Course Placement Tests

Choose printable or online version.

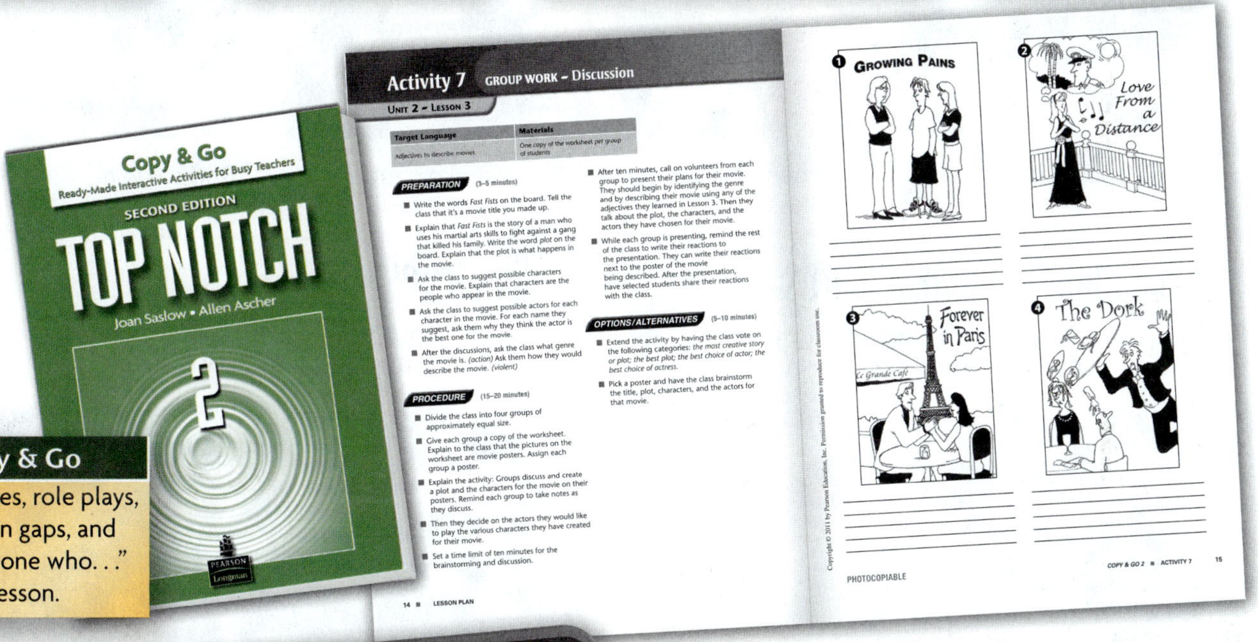

Copy & Go

Board games, role plays, information gaps, and "find someone who. . ." for every lesson.

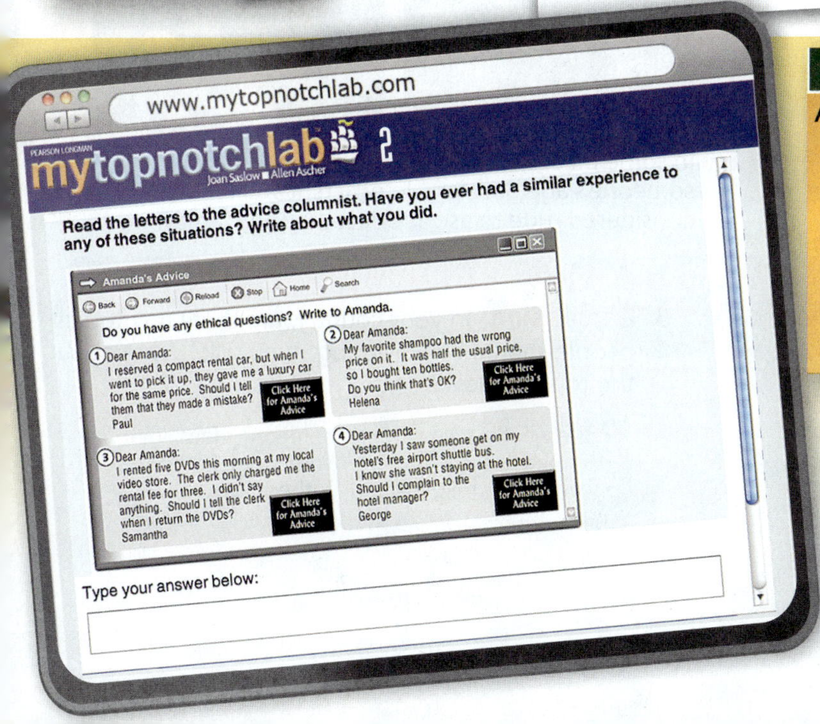

MyTopNotchLab

An optional online learning tool with:

- An interactive *Top Notch* Workbook
- Speaking and writing activities
- Pop-up grammar help
- Student's Book *Grammar Booster* exercises
- *Top Notch TV* with extensive viewing activities
- Automatically-graded achievement tests
- Easy course management and record-keeping

UNIT 1

Greetings and Small Talk

Preview

GOALS After Unit 1, you will be abl

1 Get reacquainted with someone.
2 Greet a visitor to your country.
3 Discuss gestures and customs.
4 Describe an interesting experience.

Customs Around the World

Greetings

People greet each other differently around the world.

Some people bow.

Some people kiss once. Some kiss twice.

Some shake hands.

And some hug.

Exchanging Business Cards

People have different customs for exchanging business cards around the world.

Some customs are very formal. People always use two hands and look at the card carefully.

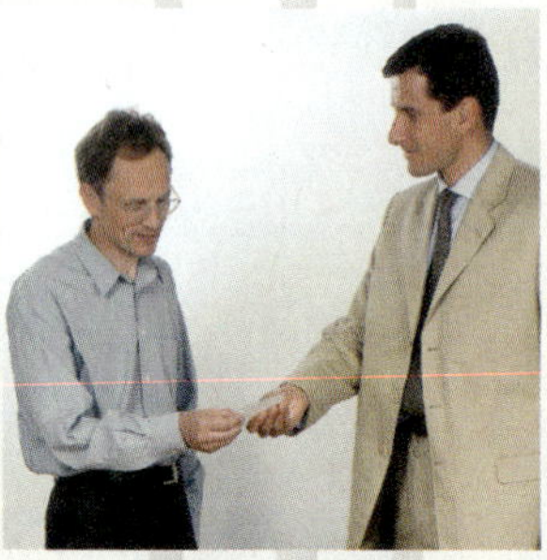

Other customs are informal. People accept a card with one hand and quickly put it in a pocket.

Small Talk

What about small talk—the topics people talk about when they don't know each other well?

In some places, it's not polite to ask about someone's age or salary. In others, it's considered rude to ask about someone's family.

A Pair work In your opinion, is there a right way and a wrong way to greet people? Explain.

B Discussion In your country, are there any topics people should avoid during small talk? What about the topics below?

- the weather
- someone's job
- someone's religion
- someone's family
- someone's home
- (other) ________

C 1:02 **Photo story** Read and listen to two people meeting in a hotel lobby.

ENGLISH FOR TODAY'S WORLD
connecting people from different cultures and language backgrounds

Leon: You look familiar. Haven't we met somewhere before?

Taka: I don't think so. I'm not from around here.

Leon: I know! Aren't you from Japan? I'm sure we met at the IT conference last week.

Taka: Of course! You're from Mexico, right?

Leon: That's right. I'm sorry. I've forgotten your name.

Taka: Kamura Takashi. But you can call me Taka.

Leon: Hi, Taka. Leon Prieto. Please call me Leon. So, what have you been up to since the conference?

Taka: Not much. Actually, I'm on my way to the airport now. I'm flying back home.

Leon: Hey, we should keep in touch. Here's my card. The conference is in Acapulco next year and I could show you around.

Taka: That would be great. I hear Acapulco's beautiful.

Leon: It was nice to see you again, Taka.

Taka: You, too.

Leon: Spanish speaker / Taka: Japanese speaker

D Focus on language Find an underlined expression in the Photo Story to match each of the following explanations.

1. You say this when you want to offer to introduce someone to a new place.
2. You say this to suggest that someone call or e-mail you in the future.
3. You say this when you're not sure if you know someone, but you think you might.
4. You say this when you want to ask about someone's recent activities.

E Think and explain Answer the questions, according to the Photo Story. Explain your answers.

1. Why does Leon begin speaking with Taka?
2. Has Taka been busy since the conference?
3. Why does Leon give Taka his business card?
4. What does Leon offer to do at the next conference?

F Pair work Write suggestions to a visitor about how to behave in your country. Then share your advice with the class.

"Never ask about a person's age or salary!"

"Please don't exchange business cards with one hand!"

Your advice

1

2

3

LESSON 1

GOAL Get reacquainted with someone

CONVERSATION MODEL

A 1:03 Read and listen to people getting reacquainted.

A: Audrey, have you met Hanah?
B: No, I haven't.
A: Hanah, I'd like you to meet Audrey.
C: Hi, Audrey. You look familiar. Have we met before?
B: I don't think so.
C: I know! Last month. You were at my sister Nicole's party.
B: Oh, that's right! How have you been?

B 1:04 **Rhythm and intonation** Listen again and repeat. Then practice the Conversation Model with a partner.

GRAMMAR *The present perfect*

Use the present perfect to talk about an indefinite time in the past.
Use the simple past tense to talk about a definite or specific time.

present perfect: indefinite time	simple past tense: definite time
I**'ve met** Bill twice.	We **met** in 1999 and again in 2004.

Form the present perfect with <u>**have**</u> **or** <u>**has**</u> **and a past participle. For regular verbs, the past participle form is the same as the simple past form:** (open → open**ed**, study → studi**ed**)

We {**'ve** / **haven't**} **met** them.   She {**'s** / **hasn't**} **called** him.

Have you **met** them?   **Has** she **called** him?
Yes, we **have**. / No, we **haven't**.   Yes, she **has**. / No, she **hasn't**.

Contractions
have met = **'ve** met
has met = **'s** met
have not met = **haven't** met
has not met = **hasn't** met

Irregular verbs

base form	simple past	past participle
be	was / were	**been**
come	came	**come**
do	did	**done**
eat	ate	**eaten**
fall	fell	**fallen**
go	went	**gone**
have	had	**had**
make	made	**made**
meet	met	**met**
see	saw	**seen**
speak	spoke	**spoken**
take	took	**taken**
write	wrote	**written**

For more irregular verb forms, open **Reference Charts** on your *ActiveBook* Self-Study Disc.

GRAMMAR BOOSTER ▸ p. 122
• *The present perfect: information questions*

A **Pair work** Complete the conversations with the present perfect or the simple past tense. Then practice the conversations with a partner.

1 A: .... our new teacher? (Jake / meet)
B: Yes, ... He .... her in the office this morning. (meet)

2 A: .... to this class before? (they / be)
B: No, ... They're new at this school.

3 A: .... in the new school restaurant? (you / eat)
B: No, ... Is it good?

4 A: .... with the school director? (your classmates / speak)
B: Yes, ... They .... with her yesterday. (speak)

5 A: .... the new language lab? (Beth / see)
B: No, ... But she .... the library. (see)

B Grammar practice Complete the message with the present perfect or the simple past tense.

FaceSpace SAVE DELETE REPLY ATTACH

Antoinetta

Birthday: June 3

Current city: Montreal

Hometown: Rome

SEARCH
INBOX
SENT

August 29 at 10:50 AM

Hi, Emilie:

I have always remembered your wonderful English classes in Rome, and when I (1 see) ________ you on FaceSpace yesterday, I (2 decide) ________ to send you a message to say hello. We (3 not see) ________ each other in years! So let me tell you what I've been up to. In 2006, I (4 move) ________ to Canada, and I'm living in Montreal right now. I'm still studying English, and I recently (5 enroll) ________ in a great language school here. I (6 travel) ________ a lot in Canada and the US, too. I (7 be) ________ to Toronto, Halifax, Boston, and New York. I (8 go) ________ back home to Rome to visit my parents last September. Sorry I (9 not call) ________ you then! Do you think my English is better now? I'm going to keep studying until I can speak as well as you! After more than three years here, I (10 fall) ________ in love with this city! Let's keep in touch. If you come to Montreal, I'd love to show you around.

Antoinetta

PRONUNCIATION *Sound reduction in the present perfect*

A 1:05 Listen to how the sound /t/ of the negative contraction "disappears." Then listen again and repeat.

1. I haven't been to that class.
2. He hasn't met his new teacher.
3. They haven't taken the test.
4. She hasn't heard the news.

B Now practice saying the sentences on your own.

NOW YOU CAN Get reacquainted with someone

Group work Adapt the Conversation Model. With two other students, make introductions and get reacquainted. Use the present perfect. Then change the situation and roles.

A: ...., have you met ....?

B: No, I haven't.

A: ...., I'd like you to meet ....

C: .... You look familiar. Have we met before?

B: ....

Ideas

You met...

- at a party
- at a meeting
- at a friend's house
- in a class
- (your own idea) ____

Don't stop!

Engage in small talk.
Talk about how the weather has been.
Ask what your partners did before class began.
Introduce other classmates.

LESSON 2

GOAL Greet a visitor to your country

VOCABULARY *Tourist activities around the world*

A 1:06 Read and listen. Then listen again and repeat.

climb Mt. Fuji

go sightseeing in New York

go to the top of the Eiffel Tower

try Korean food

take a tour of the Tower of London

take pictures of the Great Wall

B Pair work What tourist activities have you done? Which haven't you done? Use the Vocabulary and the present perfect.

"I've climbed two famous mountains."

"I haven't gone to the top of the Empire State Building in New York."

GRAMMAR *The present perfect: already, yet, ever, and before*

Use yet or already in questions about recent experiences.

Have you toured Quito **yet**? Has she **already** tried Korean barbecue?

Use already in affirmative statements. Use yet in negative statements.

I've **already** tried sushi. I haven't tried sashimi **yet**.

Use ever or before in questions about life experiences.

Have you **ever** eaten Indian food? Has she **ever** been to London?
Have you eaten Thai food **before**? Has she been to Paris **before**?

Use already or before in affirmative statements. Use have never or haven't ever in negative statements.

I've **already** tried Indian food three times, but I**'ve never** tried Thai food.
I've tried Indian food **before**, but I **haven't ever** tried Thai food.

Be careful!
You can use before in affirmative statements. But don't use ever.
Don't say:
I've ~~ever~~ been to London before.

GRAMMAR BOOSTER ▸ p. 122
- *Yet and already: expansion, common errors*
- *Ever, never, and before: use and placement*

A Grammar practice On a separate sheet of paper, use the words to write statements or questions in the present perfect.

1 (you / go sightseeing / in London / before)
2 (she / already / try / Guatemalan food)
3 (they / ever / be / to Buenos Aires)
4 (we / not take a tour of / Prague / yet)

B 1:07 **Listening comprehension** Listen to each conversation and complete the questions. Then listen again and complete the short answers.

	Questions	Short Answers
1	Has she .... of the Great Pyramids yet?	..........., she ....
2	Has he .... in Kyoto yet?	..........., he ....
3	Has she ever .... ceviche?	..........., she ....
4	Has he already .... the Pyramid of the Sun?	..........., he ....
5	Has she ever .... to Beijing before?	..........., she ....
6	Has she .... of the Forbidden City yet?	..........., she ....

The Great Pyramids • Egypt

The Pyramid of the Sun • Mexico City

C Write five questions about tourist activities in your city or country. Use yet, already, ever, and before.

Have you ever tried our seafood dishes?

The Forbidden City • Beijing, China

Ceviche • Peru

A temple • Kyoto, Japan

CONVERSATION MODEL

A 1:08 Read and listen to someone greeting a visitor.

A: Welcome to Rio. Have you ever been here before?

B: No, it's my first time. But yesterday I went to Sugarloaf. It was really beautiful.

A: That's great. Have you tried feijoada yet?

B: Feijoada? No, I haven't. What's that?

A: It's a famous Brazilian dish. I think you'll like it.

B 1:09 **Rhythm and intonation** Listen again and repeat. Then practice the Conversation Model with a partner.

Sugarloaf, Rio de Janeiro

Feijoada

NOW YOU CAN Greet a visitor to your country

A Notepadding On the notepad, write at least five activities for a tourist in your city or country.

Activity	Description
try feijoada	*It's a famous Brazilian dish.*

Activity	Description

B Pair work Change the Conversation Model to greet a visitor to your country. Use the present perfect. Suggest tourist activities in your city. Use your notepad. Then change roles.

A: Welcome to .... Have you ever been here before?

B: No, it's my first time. But yesterday I ....

A: .... Have you ....yet?

B: ....

Don't stop!
Ask about other places and tourist activities.

C Change partners Practice the conversation again, asking about other tourist activites on your notepad.

GOAL Discuss gestures and customs

BEFORE YOU READ

Pair work Discuss which hand gestures people use in your country for the expressions below. Are there any other gestures you can think of that people often use?

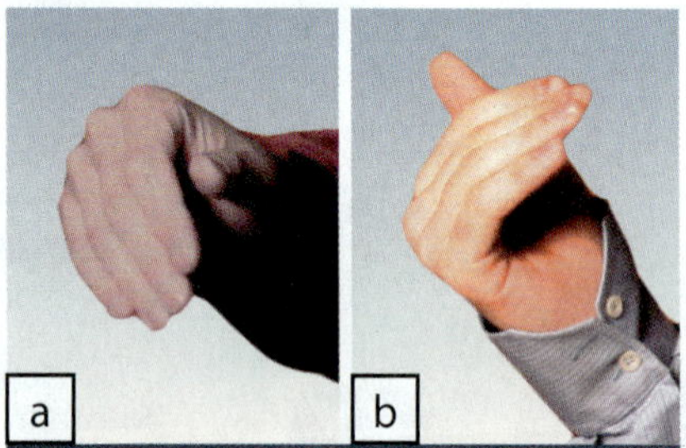

"Come with me."

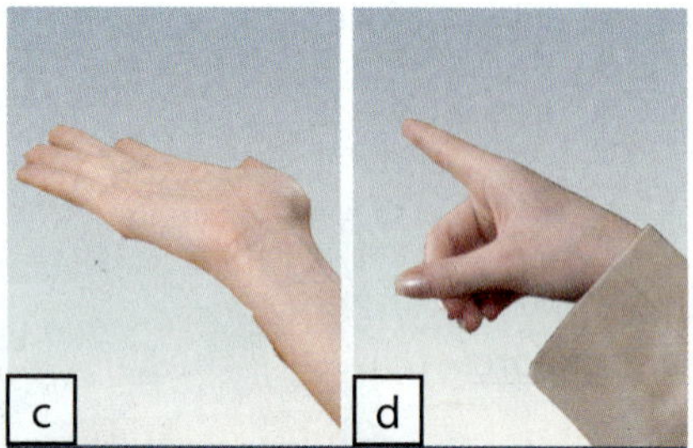

"There he is."

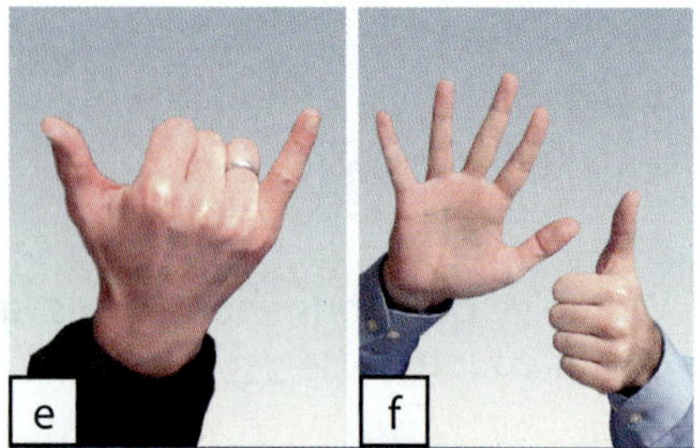

"Six."

READING

1:10

Body Talk

By Kelly Garbo

To communicate well with people of other countries, you must learn to speak well, right? Yes, but speaking isn't everything. Some experts say only thirty percent of communication comes from talking. Your gestures and other non-verbal actions matter, too.

But in different cultures, the same action can have different meanings. When you have to meet someone from a different culture, be prepared. Do you know what kind of gestures and customs are appropriate?

Let's look at shaking hands. North Americans like a firm handshake. But the French prefer a light, short handshake. If you shake a French person's hand the North American way, he or she may not like it. People in Eastern European countries and some Latino cultures prefer shorter handshakes, too. Hugging after shaking hands is also a common introduction there. Don't be surprised if a Brazilian gives you a hug. If you misinterpret gestures of introduction, your friendship may get off on the wrong foot!

Everyone around the world knows the "OK" hand gesture don't they? But in Spain, parts of South America, and Eastern Europe, the OK sign is considered rude. And if you go shopping in Japan, it means you'd like your change in coins instead of bills. In France, making the OK sign means "zero" or that something is worthless. So check before you use the OK sign to be sure it's OK!

Understanding even a few key gestures from different cultures can make you a better communicator. So next time you travel, try being culturally sensitive. Find out the local gesture and let your body talk.

Source: bellaonline.com

A Identify supporting details Check the statements that are true, according to the article. Explain your answers.

- ☐ **1** Seventy percent of communication comes from non-verbal actions.
- ☐ **2** If you don't speak someone's language, it's always safe to use gestures from your own culture.
- ☐ **3** Eastern Europeans generally don't like long handshakes.
- ☐ **4** Hugging is common during introductions in Brazil.
- ☐ **5** Japanese people think the OK sign is rude.

B Relate to personal experience Discuss the questions:
Have you ever been surprised by someone's body language on TV, in the movies, or in real life? What was the non-verbal action? What do you think it meant? Why were you surprised?

On your *ActiveBook* Self-Study Disc:
Extra Reading Comprehension Questions

NOW YOU CAN Discuss gestures and customs

A Pair work Read the travel tips about gestures and customs around the world. Compare your own customs with those described.

Travel Tips

If someone gives you a gift, thank the person and open it right away. (Ecuador)

If you want to get a server's attention, it's more polite to use eye contact rather than hand gestures. (Kenya)

If you are going to be more than 15 minutes late for a party, lunch, or dinner, you should call to explain. (United States)

If you invite someone to go to a restaurant, you should always pay for the meal. (India)

Before you enter someone's home, you should take off your shoes. (Ukraine)

When a visitor is leaving your home, you should walk with that person out the door. (Korea)

When greeting people, older people should always be greeted first. (Mongolia)

B Notepadding With a partner, choose a topic and discuss your country's customs. Then write notes about your country on the notepad.

Topic: *showing respect for older people.*
Customs: *It's not polite to disagree with an older person.*

Topic:

Customs:

Are the rules the same for both men and women? How about for young people or older people? Explain.

Topics
- showing respect to older people
- do's and don'ts for gestures
- invitations
- visiting someone's home
- giving gifts
- offering or refusing food
- touching or not touching
- (your own topic) ___

C Discussion Tell your classmates about the customs you described on your notepad. Does everyone agree?

Text-mining (optional)
Underline language in the Reading on page 8 to use in the Discussion. For example:
"Don't be surprised if …"

LESSON 4

GOAL Describe an interesting experience

BEFORE YOU LISTEN

A 1:11 **Vocabulary** • *Participial adjectives* Read and listen. Then listen again and repeat.

The safari was **fascinating**. (They were **fascinated**.)

The ski trip was **thrilling**. (They were **thrilled**.)

The sky-dive was **frightening**. (They were **frightened**.)

The food was **disgusting**. (They were **disgusted**.)

B On a separate sheet of paper, write lists of things you think are fascinating, thrilling, frightening, and disgusting.

C **Pair work** Compare your lists.

"I think eating snails is disgusting."

"Really? I've tried them and I wasn't disgusted at all."

LISTENING COMPREHENSION

A 1:12 **Listen to associate** Listen to the three interviews. Then listen again and write the number of the speaker described by each statement.

...3... **a** travels to have thrilling experiences

.... **b** describes differences in body language

.... **c** was disgusted by something

.... **d** is fascinated by other cultures

.... **e** tries to be polite

.... **f** does some things that are scary

2 Andrew Barlow

1 Nancy Sullivan

3 Mieko Nakamura

1:13

B **Listen for details** Listen again and answer the questions in complete sentences.

1 **Nancy Sullivan**

a How many countries has she visited? ....

b What did she notice about gestures in India? ....

2 **Andrew Barlow**

c What did the people in the village do to thank him? ....

d Why did he eat something he didn't want to? ....

3 **Mieko Nakamura**

e What has she done twice? ....

f How did she get to "the top of the world"? ....

NOW YOU CAN Describe an interesting experience

A **Notepadding** Answer the questions. Explain what happened. Write as many details as you can.

Have you ever been someplace that was really fascinating?

Have you ever eaten something that was really strange or disgusting?

Have you ever done something that was really thrilling or frightening?

B **Pair work** Ask your partner about the experiences on his or her notepad.

Don't stop!
Ask more questions.
Ask about other experiences.
"Have you ever ..."

Be sure to recycle this language.

climb ___
go sightseeing in ___
go to the top of ___
try ___
take a tour of ___
take pictures of ___

C **Group work** Choose one of the experiences your partner told you about. Tell your classmates about your partner's experience.

"My partner went hang gliding last year. She was frightened but it was really thrilling."

hang gliding

Review

More Practice
ActiveBook *Self-Study Disc*
grammar · vocabulary · listening
reading · speaking · pronunciatic

A 1:14 **Listening comprehension** Listen to the conversation with a tourist in Vancouver and check Yes or No. Then listen again and write the answers to the questions, using yet or already.

	Has she...	Yes	No	
1	been to the Vancouver Aquarium?	☑	☐	*Yes. She's already been to the . . .*
2	visited Gastown?	☐	☐	
3	been to the top of Grouse Mountain?	☐	☐	
4	seen the Capilano Suspension Bridge?	☐	☐	
5	tried dim sum?	☐	☐	
6	gone to the top of the Harbour Centre Tower?	☐	☐	

B Use the photos to write questions using the present perfect with ever or before. Don't use the same verb more than once.

1 ....
2 ....
3 ....
4 ....

C On a separate sheet of paper, write sentences about the topics below, using the present perfect.

1 *I've been to the top of the Taipei 101 Building.*

1 tall buildings you've been to the top of
2 cities or countries you've visited
3 foods you've tried
4 mountains or high places you've climbed

D **Writing** On a separate sheet of paper, write about one of the experiences you talked about in Lesson 4. Describe what happened, where you were, who you were with, and how you felt.

I've had a few frightening experiences in my life.
Last year, I was on vacation in . . .

1:15/1:16 **Top Notch Pop**
"Greetings and Small Talk"
Lyrics p. 149

WRITING BOOSTER ▸ p. 139
- *Avoiding run-on sentences*
- *Preparation for Exercise D*

ORAL REVIEW

Pair work

1 Create a conversation for the man and woman. Imagine the man is welcoming the woman to his city. (Choose one of the cities on the map.)

Welcome to Paris. Have you been here before?

2 Create a conversation for the three people below. Imagine they get reacquainted during a tour of Europe.

A: Have you met ___?

B: Actually, you look familiar. Have we met before?

C: Yes, I think we have. You were on the tour of . . .

3 Imagine that you are on a tour of Europe. Ask and answer questions, using the present perfect.

Have you tried crepes yet?

NOW I CAN...

- ☐ Get reacquainted with someone.
- ☐ Greet a visitor to my country.
- ☐ Discuss gestures and customs.
- ☐ Describe an interesting experience.

UNIT 2

Movies and Entertainment

Preview

GOALS After Unit 2, you will be abl

1 Apologize for being late.
2 Discuss preferences for movie genre
3 Describe and recommend movies.
4 Discuss effects of violence on viewer

» Sign In | Sign Up | Help | Feedback

NETCLIPS

Click on ▶ to preview movies before buying.
Or choose the "rent" option if you'd rather rent than buy.

Blood Diamond

Leonardo DiCaprio stars as an ex-criminal involved in the violent diamond trade during the 1999 civil war in Sierra Leone. He joins with a fisherman (Djimon Hounsou) in a common goal: to recover a pink diamond that can change both their lives. Jennifer Connelly plays the love interest as a journalist reporting on the war. An exciting yet touching story. (2006)

Download to buy

Download to rent

Catch Me if You Can

Based on a 1960s true story, *Catch Me if You Can* follows the hilarious life of a teenage con artist (DiCaprio) who pretends to be a pilot, a doctor, and a lawyer. Directed by Steven Spielberg, the movie masterfully develops the teenager's relationship with the FBI agent (Tom Hanks) who is trying to catch him. (2002)

Download to buy

Download to rent

Revolutionary Road

Based on the novel by Richard Yates, this drama examines the unhappy lives of Frank and April Wheeler (DiCaprio and Kate Winslet), a smart, talented suburban couple who have always believed they were made to do something great. The couple struggles to accept the truth that they may not be any more special than their neighbors—with tragic results. (2008)

Download to buy

Download to rent

Titanic

This 1997 blockbuster disaster movie is less the true story of the ill-fated ocean liner *Titanic* than a 194-minute love story. Rose (Kate Winslet), a wealthy but unhappy bride-to-be, falls for Jack (DiCaprio), a poor artist who gives her life meaning. The scenes of the sinking of the magnificent *Titanic* are truly frightening. A romantic epic! (1997)

Download to buy

Download to rent

More DiCaprio clips

BY GENRE

comedy
drama
action
crime
romance
disaster

BY TITLE

The Man in the Iron Mask (1998)
The Beach (2000)
Gangs of New York (2002)
The Aviator (2004)
The Departed (2006)
Body of Lies (2008)
Shutter Island (2010)
The Wolf of Wall Street (2010)
Brave New World (2011)
The Rise of Theodore Roosevelt (2011)

A Pair work Look at all the Leonardo DiCaprio movies on the website. Talk about the movies you've seen and choose the ones you'd like to see.

B Discussion Where do you like to see movies: at home or in a movie theater? Explain your reasons.

1:17

C 🔊 **Photo story** Read and listen to a conversation at a movie theater.

Anna: So, what are you in the mood for? They've got a bunch of great classic movies tonight.

Peter: They sure do. Hey, you're a big DiCaprio fan. I missed *Gangs of New York* when it was playing. Have you ever seen it?

Anna: Nope, I haven't. I've heard it's pretty violent. Frankly, I just can't take all that fighting.

Peter: Yeah. It *is* supposed to be pretty bloody. ...What else?

Anna: Well, there's *Wall-E*. They say it's spectacular. What do you think?

Peter: Hmm. To tell you the truth, I can't stand animated films. Sorry. I don't think I could handle a picture with two hours of a machine talking. I think I'd rather see something...

Peter: Hey! What about *Casablanca*?

Anna: *Casablanca*? Now you're talking! And by the way, it's my treat. You paid last time. What do you say?

Peter: It's a deal! I'll get the popcorn.

D **Focus on language** Find an underlined word or expression in the Photo Story that has a similar meaning to each of the following words and phrases.

1 "I'll pay."
2 "really don't like"
3 "To tell you the truth..."
4 "a lot of"
5 "didn't see"
6 "They say..."

E **Infer meaning** With a partner, discuss and find...

1 two different nouns that have the same meaning as "movie."
2 two different adjectives that are related to "fighting" or "killing."
3 an adjective that means "really great."

F **Think and explain** Answer each question. Then explain your answer with a sentence from the Photo Story.

1 What actor does Anna like? ....
How do you know?
Peter says, " Hey, you're a big DiCaprio fan ."

2 Did Anna see *Gangs of New York*? ....
How do you know?
She says, " ...."

3 What movie does Anna suggest? ....
How do you know?
She says, " ...."

4 Who is going to pay for the popcorn? ....
How do you know?
Peter says, " ...."

G **Pair work** Make a list of movies playing in your town. Which movies would you like to see? Which movies would you not like to see? Explain why or why not.

LESSON 1

GOAL Apologize for being late

GRAMMAR The present perfect: for and since; Other uses

Use since with a specific time or date in the past. Use for to describe a period of time.

How long have you been here? { I've been here **since eight o'clock**. (a time in the past)
I've been here **for ten minutes**. (a period of time) }

Other uses:

- with always: I've **always** wanted to see *Car Planet*.
- with ordinals, superlatives, only:
  This is **the third time** I've seen *Ping Pong*.
  It's **the best** movie I've ever seen.
  My husband has **only** seen it once.
- with lately, recently, just:
  Have you seen a good movie **recently**?
  I've **just** seen *The Beach*—what a great movie!
- with still, so far: You **still** haven't seen *Tomato Babies*? I've seen it three times **so far**!

GRAMMAR BOOSTER ▸ p. 1

- *The present perfect continuous: unfinished actions*
- *Spelling rules for the present participle: review, common erro*

A Grammar practice Choose the correct words to complete the paragraph.

I've been a big fan of Penélope Cruz (1 for / since) more than five years. I've followed her career (2 since / so far) I was in high school. That means I've watched every movie she's made (3 for / since) 1988, except for *Volver*. I (4 yet / still) haven't seen that one, but I plan to see it soon. I've (5 still / always) loved Penélope's work. I've (6 since / always) been the first person in line at the theater when her movies open. Of the movies Penélope has made (7 lately / always), the most interesting to me is *Nine*. I think it's the (8 best / still) movie she's made (9 so far / still). I've (10 always / already) seen it five times!

B Pair work Take turns asking and answering the following questions. Use the present perfect in all your answers.

1. Is there a movie you've always wanted to see?
2. Have you seen any good movies recently?
3. What's the best movie you've ever seen?
4. What's the worst movie you've ever seen?
5. How many movies have you seen so far this month?
6. Have you ever seen a movie more than once?

VOCABULARY Explanations for being late

A 1:18 Read and listen. Then listen again and repeat.

I overslept.

I missed the bus.

I couldn't get a taxi.

I couldn't find a parking space.

I got stuck in traffic.

B Pair work Think of two other explanations for being late.

1:19
C **Listening comprehension** Listen to the conversations. Complete the sentences, using the Vocabulary.

1 Ted's late because he ....
2 Maude probably ....
3 They're going to be late because they ....
4 First they .... Then they probably ....

PRONUNCIATION *Reduction of h*

1:20
Notice how the sound /h/ often disappears in present perfect questions. Read and listen. Then listen again and repeat.

1 How long have you waited?
2 Where have you been?
3 What has he heard about the film?
4 When did he buy the tickets?
5 What's her favorite movie?
6 Who's his favorite star?

CONVERSATION MODEL

1:21
A Read and listen to someone apologize for being late.

A: Have you been here long?
B: For about ten minutes.
A: Sorry I'm late. I got stuck in traffic. Did you get tickets?
B: Yes. But the 8:00 show for *The Love Boat* is sold out. I got tickets for *Paradise Island*. I hope that's OK.
A: That's fine. How much do I owe?
B: Nothing. It's on me.
A: Well, thanks! Next time it's my treat.

1:22
B **Rhythm and intonation** Listen again and repeat. Then practice the Conversation Model with a partner.

NOW YOU CAN Apologize for being late

A Add four more movies to the showtimes.

The Sun King	7:00	9:00	11:00
	7:30	9:35	[7:30 sold out]
	7:45	10:20	midnight
	8:00	11:00	[8:00 sold out]
	7:50	10:10	

B **Pair work** Personalize the Conversation Model with your movies and explanations. Then change roles.

A: Have you been here long?
B: For ....
A: Sorry I'm late. I .... Did you get tickets?
B: Yes. But .... I hope that's OK.
A: ....

Be sure to recycle this language.

___ is sold out.
We missed ___.
It started ___ minutes ago.
I've already seen ___.
That's past my bedtime!
I can't stand ___.
I'm not a(n) ___ fan.

I've heard it's ___.
It's supposed to be ___.
How much do I owe?
It's on me.
It's my treat.
What do you say?

Don't stop!
Say more about the movie.
Offer to pay.
Discuss what to do after the show.

C **Change partners** Practice the conversation again, making other changes.

LESSON 2

GOAL Discuss preferences for movie genres

VOCABULARY *Movie genres*

1:23

A Read and listen. Then listen again and repeat.

an action film

a horror film

a science-fiction film

an animated film

a comedy

a drama

a documentary

a musical

B Pair work Compare your favorite movies for each genre.

"My favorite animated film is *Shrek*."

1:24

C Listening comprehension Listen to the conversations about movies. Write the genre for each movie. Then circle the movie if the people decided to see it.

Movie	Genre
1 *The Bottom of the Sea*	
2 *Tango in Tap Shoes*	
3 *The Ant Who Wouldn't Die*	
4 *Chickens Never Wear Shoes*	
5 *Goldilocks Grows Up*	
6 *The Equalizer*	
7 *Twelve Angry Women*	
8 *City Under the Sea*	

D Discussion Which movies sound good to you? Listen again if necessary. Explain your choices.

GRAMMAR *Would rather + base form*

State preferences with would rather / would rather not and the base form of a verb.

She'**d rather see** a less violent film.
We'**d rather not see** a horror film.

Use than with would rather to contrast preferences.

I'**d rather rent** a movie **than** go to the theater.
They'**d rather go** to a Woody Allen film **than** a Martin Scorsese film.

Questions

Would you **rather see** *Casablanca* or *Wall-E*?
Which **would** they **rather see**—a comedy or a drama?
What **would** you **rather do**—see a play or a movie?

Short answers

Would you rather stay home? Yes, **we would.** NOT Yes, ~~we'd rather~~.
Would you like to see a movie? Actually, we'**d rather not.** We're too busy.

I / He / We / They **'d rather** **see** a musical. / **not go out** tonight.

Be careful!
Don't use to after would rather.
NOT He'd rather ~~to~~ see a comedy.

GRAMMAR BOOSTER ▸ p. 124
• *Expressing preferences: review*

A Grammar practice Complete each response, using 'd rather or 'd rather not and expressing a different preference.

1 "I'd love to see a drama tonight." YOU Actually, ...
2 "I'm in the mood for a horror film." YOU Actually, ...
3 "Let's get tickets for the late show." YOU Actually, ...
4 "Ben told me you wanted to rent a movie." YOU Actually, ...
5 "Would you like to see a comedy?" YOU Actually, ...
6 "How about some dinner after the film?" YOU Actually, ...

B Pair work Practice the conversations in Exercise A. Take turns reading the items.

CONVERSATION MODEL

1:25
A Read and listen to people discuss their movie preferences.

A: What would you rather see—a classic or a new release?
B: It doesn't matter to me. You choose.
A: Well, what would you say to a documentary?
B: Hmm. To tell you the truth, I'm not that big on documentaries.
A: What about a comedy?
B: That works for me.

Describing preferences

☺	😐	☹
I love ___s. ___s are great. ___s are my favorite.	I can take them or leave them. ___s are OK.	I'm not that big on ___s. I don't like ___s. I can't stand ___s.

1:26
B **Rhythm and intonation** Listen again and repeat. Then practice the Conversation Model with a partner.

NOW YOU CAN Discuss preferences for movie genres

A Pair work Personalize the Conversation Model, expressing your own preferences in movie genres. Then change roles.

A: What would you rather see—........ or ....?
B: It doesn't matter to me. You choose.
A: Well, what would you say to ....?
B: Hmm. To tell you the truth, I ....
A: What about ....?
B: ....

Be sure to recycle this language.

It's on me. It's my treat. I'm sorry I'm late. Have you been here long? Have you ever seen ___? I missed it.	Actually, ___. Frankly, ___. I'm not that big on ___s. I can't stand ___s.

B Change partners Change the conversation from a video store to in front of a movie theater. Talk about specific movies.

LESSON 3

GOAL Describe and recommend movies

BEFORE YOU LISTEN

A 1.27 **Vocabulary** • ***Adjectives to describe movies*** Read and listen. Then listen again and repeat.

funny something that makes you laugh

hilarious very, very funny

silly not serious; almost stupid

boring not interesting

romantic about love

weird very strange or unusual, in a negative way

unforgettable something you are going to remember

thought-provoking something that makes you think

violent bloody; with a lot of fighting and killing

B **Pair work** Write the title of a movie for each adjective. Then compare choices.

a funny movie	
a hilarious movie	
a silly movie	
a boring movie	
a romantic movie	
a weird movie	
an unforgettable movie	
a thought-provoking movie	
a violent movie	

LISTENING COMPREHENSION

A 1:28 **Listen for main ideas** Listen to the movie reviewer. Write a check next to the movies he recommends and write an X next to the ones he doesn't.

1 ☐ *Popcorn* **2** ☐ *The Vacation* **3** ☐ *Aquamundo* **4** ☐ *Wolf Babies*

B 1:29 **Infer meaning** Listen carefully to each movie review again. Based on the reviewer's opinion, circle one or more adjectives to describe each movie.

1 *Popcorn* (weird / funny / boring)

2 *The Vacation* (romantic / violent / unforgettable)

3 *Aquamundo* (boring / violent / thought-provoking)

4 *Wolf Babies* (violent / boring / hilarious)

C 1:30 **Dictation** Listen to the following excerpts from the reviews. Complete each statement, based on what you hear.

POPCORN ★

① First up is *Popcorn*, a new .... starring David Bodine and Judy Crabbe. ② Unfortunately, *Popcorn* is a complete waste of ....

THE VACATION ★ ★ ★ ★ ★

③ Our next film, *The Vacation*, is a well-acted and .... ④ I highly .... wonderful ....

AQUAMUNDO ★ ★ ★

⑤ *Aquamundo* is no .... film it's based on real scientific research. ⑥ A .... film. Don't ....

WOLF BABIES ★ ★ ★

⑦ Adults will find the story .... , but children won' forget these .... , scary scenes for a long time

NOW YOU CAN Describe and recommend movies

A Pair work Read the short movie reviews and choose the movie you think sounds the most interesting. Then compare movie choices. Explain your reasons.

WHAT'S YOUR ALL-TIME FAVORITE MOVIE?

I've just seen ***Casablanca*** for the hundredth time, at least. It's the most romantic movie in the world, and there's no movie I would rather see. Humphrey Bogart and Ingrid Bergman star as former lovers who meet after many years. They're still in love and have to make some difficult choices. The ending is unforgettable and always makes me cry. This movie was made in 1942, but it's always "new." I guess that's what makes it a classic.

The Hunt for Red October, starring Alec Baldwin and Sean Connery, is one of my all-time favorites. It was made in 1990, so it's a little dated now, but it's still one of the most exciting action movies ever made. This fast-paced thriller kept me on the edge of my seat from beginning to end. I hope you go to see this movie, so I don't want to give away the plot, but the movie is about a Soviet nuclear submarine that comes very close to American waters. The crew of an American submarine must decide: Is the submarine trying to escape the Soviet Union—or start a nuclear war?

Wow! I've just seen ***Phantom of the Opera***. I once saw the musical on stage, but it really comes alive on screen. The Andrew Lloyd Webber music is stunningly beautiful, and the tragic love story is always unforgettable. This musical isn't for everybody. Some people find the story kind of weird, but I love it.

I've just seen ***Tootsie***. What a great movie—perhaps one of the most hilarious romantic comedies of all time. Dustin Hoffman stars as out-of-work actor Michael Dorsey, who dresses as a woman to get a part on a TV soap opera. But complications arise when he falls in love with his co-star, Jessica Lange, who doesn't know Michael is a man. If you want a good laugh, be sure to see this film!

B Notepadding Write notes about a movie you've seen recently. (It's OK if you don't have all the information.)

Title of film:

Genre:

Stars:

Director or producer:

Adjectives that describe the movie:

What the movie is about:

C Group work Describe and recommend the movies on your notepads.

Don't stop!
Ask questions.

Be sure to recycle this language.

Questions
Was it (funny)?
Who was in it?
What kind of movie was it?
Do you recommend it?
What was it about?

More adjectives

thrilling	exciting
fascinating	great
frightening	interesting
disgusting	bloody

Text-mining (optional)
Underline language in the reviews in Exercise A to use in Group Work.
For example:
"___ stars as a / an ___."

LESSON 4

GOAL Discuss effects of violence on viewers

BEFORE YOU READ

Warm-up At what age do you think it's safe to permit children to see violent movies and TV shows? Explain.

READING

1:31

Can Violent Movies or TV Programs Harm Children?

A number of scientific studies have reported that watching violence can make children more aggressive. According to the research, two kinds of programs and movies encourage aggressive behavior in young children more than others: (1) realistic violent action programs and movies and (2) violent cartoons.

One disturbing conclusion is that the effects of violent viewing last for many years. One study showed that children who watched violent TV programs when they were 8 years old were more likely to behave aggressively at age 18. Furthermore, as adults they were more likely to be convicted of violent crimes, such as child abuse and murder.

Studies have also demonstrated that watching violent movies and TV shows can affect children's attitudes towards violence in the world around them. Children who watch a lot of violence become less sensitive to it in the real world. If children find violence normal, they may accept more violence in society or even commit violent acts themselves.

Very often, characters in movies and on television who commit violent crimes are not sorry for their actions and don't face consequences or punishment. When children see fictional characters like these, they learn that doing bad things is OK. For children, who are growing and developing, this is a bad message.

So what can we do? With young children, we have the power to control the TV programs and movies they watch, so we can protect them from seeing any violence at all. However, with older children it's impossible to completely prevent their exposure to violence. But we can try to limit the number of hours they spend watching it. And when children have seen a violent film or TV show, it's important to discuss it with them, to help them understand that violence is not a normal part of life.

Information source: education.pitt.edu

A Confirm content Discuss the following questions, using the information in the article. Then share your answers with the class.

1 Research has found that TV and movie violence can hurt children. What are some ways that viewing violence can affect children?
2 What kinds of programs and movies are most harmful?
3 Some studies show that viewing violence can have long-term effects, lasting for many years. What are some of the effects that studies have shown?
4 What bad "message" can come from violent programs and movies?
5 What suggestions does the article make to help parents prevent the bad effects of violent TV programs and movies in very young children? In older children?

B Evaluate ideas Do you agree with the article that "violence is not a normal part of life"? Explain your answer.

On your *ActiveBook* Self-Study Disc:
Extra Reading Comprehension Questions

NOW YOU CAN Discuss effects of violence on viewers

A Complete the chart with three films or television shows you know. Rate the level of violence from 0 to 3, with 3 being the most violent.

Title	Medium	Level of Violence
Gangs of New York	film	3

0 = not violent, 1 = somewhat violent, 2 = violent, 3 = ultra violent

B Notepadding Write notes about the most violent film or TV show on your chart.

Should children see it? Why? / Why not?

Is it OK for adults to see it? Why? / Why not?

Text-mining (optional)
Underline language in the Reading on page 22 to use on your notepad. For example:
"According to (the research), …"

C Discussion Discuss the effects of violence on viewers. Use the information from your notepad to help you express your ideas. Here are some questions to consider in your discussion:

- In your opinion, are there some people who should not see violent movies? If so, who?
- Is the effect of viewing violence the same in children and adults?
- Does violence encourage adults to behave aggressively?

"**I think** violent movies can make people violent. They see violence and they go out and do the same thing they see in the movie."

"**I disagree. I feel** …"

"**I agree** …"

Review

More Practice
ActiveBook *Self-Study Disc*
grammar • vocabulary • listening
reading • speaking • pronunciatio

1:32

A Listening comprehension Listen to the conversation about movies. Check the correct description of each movie.

1

☐ a romantic film
☐ a documentary about Brazil
☐ a horror movie

2

☐ an animated police story
☐ a weird love story
☐ an unforgettable comedy

3

☐ an unforgettable movie
☐ a weird police story
☐ an animated children's film

4

☐ a documentary about cooking ham
☐ a musical tragedy
☐ a silly comedy

5

☐ a documentary
☐ a movie only for adults
☐ an animated musical

6
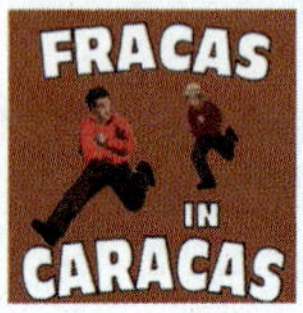

☐ a comedy
☐ an animated film
☐ a drama

B Complete the conversations. Choose the correct verbs and adverbial expressions, and write the movie genres.

1 A: (Have you seen / Did you see) a good .... (just / lately)?
B: To tell you the truth, no. But last night (we've seen / we saw) a great ....

2 A: How many times (have they seen / did they see) *War of the Worlds*?
B: That remake of the old .... movie? I think (they saw it / they've seen it) twice (still / so far).

3 A: Sally is such a .... fan. How long (has she waited / did she wait) for this film to come out on DVD?
B: She's waited (for / since) at least six months.

4 A: I (didn't see / haven't seen) a .... as good as *Twelve Angry Men*.
B: Really? I (lately / still) (didn't see / haven't seen) it.

C Complete each statement or question with <u>for</u> or <u>since</u>.

1 That film has played at the Metroplex .... two weeks.
2 *The Talking Parrot* has been available on DVD .... last Tuesday.
3 I've loved animated movies .... I was a child.
4 Have you been here .... more than an hour?
5 I've been a fan of science fiction movies .... over thirty years.
6 I've been in the ticket line .... 6:30!

1:33/1:34
Top Notch Pop
"Better Late Than Never"
Lyrics p.149

D Writing Write two paragraphs about violence in movies and on TV. Explain why some people think it's harmful and why others think it isn't.

WRITING BOOSTER ▸ p. 140
- *Paragraphs*
- *Topic sentences*
- *Preparation for Exercise D*

ORAL REVIEW

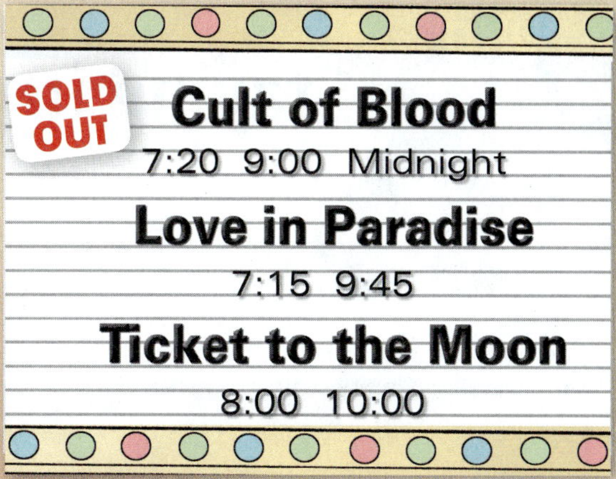

Pair work

1 With a partner, guess the genre of the three movies. Imagine what the movies are about and choose actors to star in the movies. Present your ideas to the class. Use the following as a model.

"Love in Paradise" is a romantic film. We think the movie is about a man and a woman who meet on vacation in Hawaii. They fall in love. We chose Brad Pitt and Angelina Jolie to star in the film.

2 Create a conversation for one of the couples. Say as much as you can. For example:

It's 7:30. Did we miss "Love in Paradise"?

NOW I CAN...

- ☐ Apologize for being late.
- ☐ Discuss preferences for movie genres.
- ☐ Describe and recommend movies.
- ☐ Discuss effects of violence on viewers.

UNIT 3

Staying in Hotels

Preview

GOALS After Unit 3, you will be able

1. Check into a hotel.
2. Leave and take a message.
3. Request housekeeping services.
4. Choose a hotel.

Top Notch Hotels

http://www.topnotchhotels.com

TOP NOTCH HOTELS

Top Notch Hotels Online Reservations

Luxembourg

Hong Kong

San Diego

Click on your choices. Then check availability.

Date of Arrival: July 7

Date of Departure: July 14

Number of Guests

Adults: 2

Children: 2

Smoking:

Non-smoking: X

Room Type:

Type of Bed:

Check Availability

Room Type

Single

Double

Suite

Type of Bed

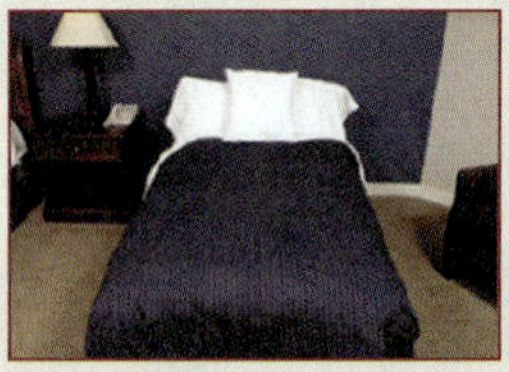
Twin

Queen-size

King-size

Rollaway

Hotel Services

We'll never let you down!

- 24-hour room service
- In-room minibar
- Free Internet service
- Full-service business center
- Laundry / Shoe-shine service
- Free airport shuttle
- Wake-up service
- Fitness / Exercise room
- Pool and sauna
- Babysitting service
- Magazine / Gift shop
- Concierge
- Currency exchange
- Baggage / Bell service
- Multilingual staff

2:02

A **Vocabulary** • ***Hotel room types and features*** Read and listen. Then listen again and repeat.

1 smoking
2 non-smoking
3 a single room
4 a double room
5 a suite
6 a twin bed
7 a queen-size bed
8 a king-size bed
9 a rollaway bed

B **Pair work** Have you—or has someone you know—ever stayed at a hotel? Tell your partner about the hotel features and services.

C 2:03 **Photo story** Read and listen to someone checking out of a hotel.

ENGLISH FOR TODAY'S WORLD
connecting people from different cultures and language backgrounds

Guest: Good morning. I'm checking out of Room 604.
Clerk: I'll be happy to help you with that. Was your stay satisfactory?
Guest: Yes. Very nice. Thanks.
Clerk: Did you have anything from the minibar last night?
Guest: Just a bottle of spring water.
Clerk: OK. Let me add that to your bill.

Clerk: And would you like to put this on your Vista card?
Guest: Yes, I would, please.
Clerk: Here you go, ma'am. Thank you for staying at the Top Notch Hotel. Will you be taking the shuttle to the airport?
Guest: Yes, I will.

Clerk: Well, the next shuttle will be arriving shortly. I'd better ask the bellman to give you a hand with your luggage.
Guest: Thanks. Actually, I'd like to pick up a paper at the newsstand. I'll just be a minute.
Clerk: No problem. The bellman will let you know when the shuttle's here.

Guest: Korean speaker

D Focus on language Find an underlined word or expression in the Photo Story with the same meaning as each of the following.

1 pay with **2** help **3** leaving **4** OK **5** only **6** soon

E Think and explain All the following statements are false. Explain how you know they are false.

1. The guest is staying for a few more days.
2. The guest has complaints about the hotel.
3. The guest pays the bill in cash.
4. The shuttle is arriving in an hour.

"The guest says, 'I'm checking out.'"

F Pair work Match each picture with a hotel service from the website on page 26. Then explain which services are important and which are not.

"Wake-up service is important. If you oversleep, you can miss a meeting or a tour."

1 ....

2 ....

3 ....

4 ....

5 ....

6 ....

7 ....

8 ....

9 ....

LESSON 1

GOAL Check into a hotel

GRAMMAR *had better*

Contractions
had better = **'d better**
had better not = **'d better not**
Note: In spoken English, had better is almost always contracted.

Use had better and the base form of a verb to warn of a possible negative result. It is a stronger form of advice than should.

They**'d better make** a reservation right away. (The hotel is almost full.)
You**'d better not check out** late. (There is a late-checkout fee.)

Remember: To give a suggestion or advice, use should and the base form of a verb.

You **should make** reservations right away.
She **shouldn't forget** her passport.

The negative form shouldn't is more common in questions than had better.

Shouldn't we **call** the airline first? { We**'d better**. There could be delays. / We**'d better not**. There's no time. }

GRAMMAR BOOSTER ▸ p. 125

- *Obligation: have to / must, common errors*
- *Suggestions and advice: could / should / ought to / had better*
- *Expectation: be supposed to*

A Grammar practice Complete the conversations. Use a verb from the box and a contraction of had better or had better not, depending on the meaning.

arrive	ask	be	call	hurry	walk

1 A: Is the gift shop still open?
B: Yes, it is. But you .... It closes in five minutes.

2 A: When does the sales meeting begin?
B: At 2:00 sharp. We .... late.

3 A: Do you think I could walk to the museum from here?
B: Well, it looks like rain. You .... You should take a taxi instead.

4 A: Do you think we could get a table at Carlo's for dinner on Friday?
B: Well, it gets pretty busy. You .... the concierge to make a reservation for you.

5 A: Hello, front desk? I'm trying to connect to the Internet but I can't seem to get online.
B: I'm so sorry. I .... the business center for you. They can send someone up to check it.

6 A: Is the fitness center open early tomorrow?
B: Yes. It opens at 7:00. But you .... early. It gets very crowded after 7:30.

B Find the grammar Look at the Photo Story on page 27 again. Circle one use of had better. Explain the possible negative result, using could.

CONVERSATION MODEL

A 2:04 Read and listen to someone checking into a hotel.

A: Hi. I'm checking in. The name's Baker.

B: Let's see. That's a double for two nights. Non-smoking?

A: That's right.

B: May I have your credit card?

A: Here you go. By the way, is the restaurant still open?

B: It is. But you'd better hurry. It closes at 9:00.

B 2:05 **Rhythm and intonation** Listen again and repeat. Then practice the Conversation Model with a partner.

C 2:06 **Listening comprehension** Listen to guests checking into a hotel. Complete the information about what each guest needs.

	Type of bed(s)	Non-smoking?	Bell service?
1		☐	☐
2		☐	☐
3		☐	☐
4		☐	☐

NOW YOU CAN Check into a hotel

A Pair work Change the Conversation Model to role-play checking into a hotel. Discuss room and bed types and ask about hotel facilities. Imagine the time is now 8:30 P.M. Use the pictures or your own ideas. Then change roles.

A: Hi, I'm checking in. The name's ....

B: Let's see. That's a .... for .... night(s). Non-smoking?

A: ....

B: May I have your credit card?

A: .... By the way, is the .... still open?

B: ....

B Change partners Practice the conversation again. Discuss other room and bed types and hotel facilities.

LESSON 2

GOAL Leave and take a message

CONVERSATION MODEL

2:07

A Read and listen to someone leave a message.

A: Hello? I'd like to speak to Anne Smith. She's a guest.

B: I'll ring that room for you . . .
I'm sorry. She's not answering. Would you like to leave a message?

A: Yes. Please tell her Tim Klein called.
I'll meet her at the hotel at three this afternoon.

B: Is that all?

A: Yes, thanks.

2:08

B **Rhythm and intonation** Listen again and repeat. Then practice the Conversation Model with a partner.

GRAMMAR *The future with will*

Use will or won't and the base form of a verb to talk about future plans.

He **will call** back tomorrow.
We **won't be able to** join you for lunch.
Will she **meet** us at the restaurant?
Will they **take** a taxi to the hotel?

Note: will / won't be able to has the same meaning as can / can't.

We **won't be able to join** you for lunch. = We **can't join** you for lunch.

Remember: You can also talk about the future with be going to, the present continuous, or the simple present tense.

I'**m going to call** again at 4:00.
They'**re meeting** at noon at the hotel.
She **arrives** on PanAir Flight 24 tomorrow.

Contractions
I will = **I'll**
she will = she**'ll**
they will = they**'ll**
He will not = He **won't**

GRAMMAR BOOSTER ▸ p. 127
- *Other uses of will*
- *Will vs. be going to*

A **Find the grammar** Look at the Conversation Model again. Circle two uses of will.

B **Grammar practice** Complete the messages, using will or won't and the base form of the verb. Use a contraction when possible.

1 Please tell Ms. Yalmaz .... (I / call) back later.

2 Please give Mr. Ballinger this message:
.... (We / not / be) at the Clayton Hotel until after 5:00.

3 Could you please tell the concierge .... (I / need) a dinner reservation for four at the Three Seasons tonight at 7:00?

4 Tell Ms. Harris .... (her brother / not / be able to) pick her up at the airport before 6:00, please.

5 Tell everyone .... (the conference call / start) at 3:00 tomorrow, London time.

6 Could you please tell Mrs. Park .... (she / have to) come in early tomorrow?

2:09

C **Listening comprehension** Listen to the phone messages. Then listen again and complete each message slip, according to the information you hear. Use the future with will in each message.

1

PHONE MESSAGE

FOR: *Judy Diller*

FROM: ☑ Mr. ☐ Ms. ☐ Mrs. ☐ Miss *Pearl*

☐ Please call ☐ Will call again

☐ Wants to see you ☐ Returned your call

Message: *He'll be . . .*

2

PHONE MESSAGE

FOR: *HANK PITT*

FROM: ☐ Mr. ☐ Ms. ☐ Mrs. ☐ Miss

☐ Please call ☐ Will call again

☐ Wants to see you ☐ Returned your call

Message:

3

PHONE MESSAGE

FOR: *Collin Mack*

FROM: ☐ Mr. ☐ Ms. ☐ Mrs. ☐ Miss

☐ Please call ☐ Will call again

☐ Wants to see you ☐ Returned your call

Message:

4

PHONE MESSAGE

FOR: *Patricia Carlton*

FROM: ☐ Mr. ☐ Ms. ☐ Mrs. ☐ Miss

☐ Please call ☐ Will call again

☐ Wants to see you ☐ Returned your call

Message:

PRONUNCIATION *Contractions with will*

2:10

A Notice that each contraction is one syllable. Read and listen. Then listen again and repeat.

1 I'll call back later.
2 She'll be at the Frank Hotel.
3 He'll bring his laptop to the meeting.
4 We'll need a taxi.
5 You'll have to leave at 6:30.
6 They'll meet you in twenty minutes.

B Look at the message slips you wrote in Exercise C above. Read each message aloud, using the correct pronunciation of the contracted form of will.

NOW YOU CAN Leave and take a message

A **Frame your ideas** On a separate sheet of paper, write four messages you could leave someone.

B **Pair work** Change the Conversation Model, using your own messages.Your partner completes the message slip. Then change roles.

A: Hello? I'd like to speak to ....

B: I'm sorry. .... Would you like to leave a message?

A: Yes. Please tell ....

B: Is that all?

A: ....

Don't stop!

- Leave another message.
- Confirm that you've understood the message correctly.
- Ask for more information.

WHILE YOU WERE OUT . . .

FOR:

☐ Mr. ☐ Ms. ☐ Mrs. ☐ Miss ________ called.

Phone:

☐ Please call back

☐ Will call again

Message:

Be sure to recycle this language.

How do you spell your last name?
Could you please spell that for me?
Could you please repeat that?
What's your ___ ?

C **Change partners** Leave other messages.

LESSON 3

GOAL Request housekeeping services

BEFORE YOU LISTEN

2:11

A **Vocabulary** • ***Hotel room amenities and services*** Read and listen. Then listen again and repeat.

We need...

extra towels.

extra hangers.

skirt hangers.

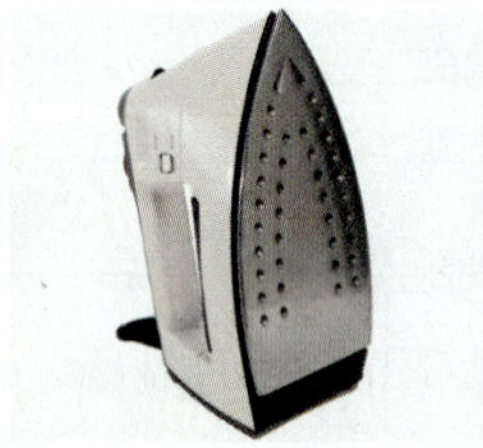

an iron.

a hair dryer.

Could someone...

make up the room?

turn down the beds?

pick up the laundry?

bring up a newspaper?

take away the dishes?

B **Expand the vocabulary** Complete the statements with other items you know. Then compare items with a partner.

1 We need extra glasses and coffee cups.
2 We also need ....
3 Could someone pick up my ....?
4 Could someone bring up ....?
5 Could someone take away the ....?

Ideas
- dirty towels
- breakfast / lunch / dinner
- bags / luggage
- a coffee maker
- a rollaway bed
- laundry bags
- (your own idea) ___

LISTENING COMPREHENSION

2:12

A **Listen for main ideas** Decide if the guests are satisfied or not. Then explain your answers.

Room 586
☐ Satisfied
☐ Not satisfied

Room 587
☐ Satisfied
☐ Not satisfied

2:13

B **Listen for details** Listen again and complete each statement.

Room 586 The guest wants someone to take away ...., bring up .... and ...., and pick up ....

Room 587 The guest wants someone to .... the ...., bring up ...., and .... the ....

NOW YOU CAN Request housekeeping services

A Pair work Look at the pictures. With a partner, discuss what you think each guest is saying.

B Pair work Role-play a telephone conversation between one of the guests and hotel staff. Use your ideas from Exercise A. Then change roles. Start like this:

A: Hello. Room service. How can I help you?
B: Hi, I'd like to order . . .

Be sure to recycle this language.

Hotel staff
Hello, (business center).
Is everything OK?
What's the problem?
I'm sorry to hear that.
Let me check.
Certainly.
You'd better hurry.

Hotel services
Internet service
business center
wake-up service
bell service

Hotel guest
Is the ___ still open?
What time does the ___ close / open?
Could someone ___ ?
Can I make a reservation for ___ ?
The ___ isn't / aren't working.
The ___ won't turn on.
I need ___ .
I'd like to order ___ .
I'd like to leave a message for ___ .
That would be great.

Don't stop!
- Complain about other problems.
- Ask for a wake-up call.
- Ask about hotel services.
- Leave a message for another hotel guest.

LESSON 4

GOAL Choose a hotel

BEFORE YOU READ

Explore your ideas What do you think is the best way to get information about a hotel?

- ☐ by word of mouth
- ☐ from an online hotel booking service
- ☐ from a travel guide book
- ☐ from a travel agency
- ☐ other ....

READING

2:14

WHERE TO STAY IN NEW YORK

New York City has some of the best hotels in the world—and, believe it or not, some are not too expensive. Here are our picks for "the best of the best."

$$$$ VERY EXPENSIVE | $$$ EXPENSIVE | $$ MODERATELY PRICED | $ BUDGET

Most Famous Hotel

The Plaza Hotel $$$

Located at the southeast corner of New York's fabulous Central Park, The Plaza is as near as it gets to the best shopping along New York's famous Fifth Avenue. This 1907 hotel, with its beautiful fountain, is a famous location in many popular movies and books. Long the choice of the rich and famous.

4 restaurants, full-service spa and health club, concierge, car-rental desk, business center, 24-hour room service

Most Interesting Hotel

Hotel Chelsea $$

If you're looking for the usual, go elsewhere. But if you're looking for atmosphere—the New York of artists, actors, and writers—this is the place. Artists and writers live here, even today. The rooms in this 1884 Victorian hotel are simple but generally large. Everything is clean, but don't expect new.

Note: Not all rooms have air-conditioning. No laundry or room service, but the staff will take your clothes to the cleaners for you or help you order out for food.

Restaurant, bell service

For the Budget-Minded

Hotel Pennsylvania $
A huge hotel and a great value. Only ten blocks south of Times Square. Traveling with your dog or cat? Pets are welcome.

The Habitat Hotel $
Built in 1999, offers inexpensive—but small—rooms with style. Near shopping.

The Hotel Newton $
Even though it's located on the Upper West Side, far from many of New York's most popular attractions, this inexpensive hotel features large clean rooms and firm beds for a good night's sleep. No pets.

The Lucerne $
Comfort and service but without the high prices. Large rooms. Great for kids.

Casablanca Hotel $
Free breakfast, coffee, tea, and cookies all day. Free passes to a nearby health club. Small rooms. Unusual Moroccan theme.

Best Service at a Low Price

The Broadway Inn $$

Impeccably clean and very comfortable, this hotel is a real winner. Suites can be a great deal—with sofa, microwave, mini-fridge, and lots of closet space. Located in noisy Broadway's Theater District, the hotel is peaceful and quiet inside. Best of all are the attentive staff who work hard to make their guests happy.

Note: This hotel has no elevators.

2 restaurants next door, concierge, fax, copy service

Best Health Club

The Peninsula-New York $$$$

This is really a place to see. High-tech rooms with remote-control lighting, music, TV, and air-conditioning—even in the bathrooms! As a matter of fact, these are the most beautiful hotel bathrooms in New York City. Wonderful food and a very helpful concierge desk. ("We'll do anything guests ask, as long as it's legal!") And on the roof you'll find one of the biggest and best spa and health clubs anywhere.

Valet parking, 2 restaurants, business center, 24-hour room service, in-room massage

Source: Adapted from *Frommer's New York City*

A Draw conclusions Write statements with 'd better or 'd better not and the name of a hotel from the Reading. You may include more than one hotel.

1 Stella Myer likes to travel, but she is 70 years old. She has some difficulty with stairs.
She'd better not stay at the . . . .

2 On his vacations, Carl Ryan likes to stay near the Theater District.
....

3 Mark and Nancy Birdsall are traveling with their kids. ....

4 Lucy Lee loves a hotel that is very comfortable and offers a lot of services.
....

5 At home, Burt and Susan Rey are very active and they go to a gym every day. They like to continue exercising when they're on vacation. ....

6 James Kay always travels with his dog, Louie. ....

B Identify supporting details Compare responses in Exercise A with a partner. If you disagree, explain why you chose a particular hotel.

On your *ActiveBook* Self-Study Disc:
Extra Reading Comprehension Questions

NOW YOU CAN Choose a hotel

A Frame your ideas What's important to you in choosing a hotel? Rate the following factors on a scale of 1 to 5.

not important ⟷ very important

price	1 –	2 –	3 –	4 –	5
room size	1 –	2 –	3 –	4 –	5
cleanliness	1 –	2 –	3 –	4 –	5
location	1 –	2 –	3 –	4 –	5
service	1 –	2 –	3 –	4 –	5
amenities	1 –	2 –	3 –	4 –	5
atmosphere	1 –	2 –	3 –	4 –	5

B Pair work Find each of the hotels from the Reading on the map. Discuss the advantages and disadvantages of each. Then choose a hotel.

"The Casablanca Hotel sounds like it has a lot of atmosphere. It's inexpensive and the location is good."

Text-mining (optional)
Underline language in the Reading on page 34 to use in the Pair Work.
For example: "If you're looking for…"

C Survey and discussion Take a survey of how many classmates chose each hotel. Discuss and explain your choices.

"Most of us chose the Hotel Newton because…"

Review

More Practice
ActiveBook Self-Study Disc
grammar • vocabulary • listening
reading • speaking • pronunciation

A 2:15 **Listening comprehension** Listen to the phone conversations in a hotel. Then listen again and complete each statement, using words from the box.

babysitting	bell	box	dinner	hangers	make up the room
laundry	room	shoeshine	towels	wake-up	turn down the beds

1 She wants someone to bring up .... She also needs .... service.
2 He needs .... service. And he wants someone to bring up extra ....
3 She wants someone to .... , and she wants someone to bring up extra ....
4 He needs .... service and .... service.

B What hotel room type or feature should each guest ask for? Explain your answers.

2:16/2:17 **Top Notch Pop** "Checking Out" Lyrics p. 149

1 Ms. Gleason is traveling alone. She doesn't need much space. ..*a single room*.........
2 Mr. and Mrs. Vanite and their twelve-year-old son Boris are checking into a room with one king-sized bed. ....
3 Mike Krause plans to use his room for business meetings with important customers. ....
4 George Nack is a big man and he's very tall. He needs a good night's sleep for an important meeting tomorrow. ....
5 Paul Krohn's company wants him to save some money by sharing a room with a colleague. ....

C Read each situation and write your own strong advice, using contractions of <u>had better</u> or <u>had better not</u>.

1 It's raining. Mona is going outside.
YOU *She'd better take a raincoat because she...*..........
2 It takes Ms. Grant 30 minutes to walk to work. She has to be there in 15 minutes.
YOU ....
3 Mr. Wang is going to take an English test tomorrow. If he does well, he can get a better job.
YOU ....
4 Karl works really hard. He hasn't had a vacation in three years.
YOU ....
5 Marie and Paul Handel like quiet hotels. The World Hotel is very noisy.
YOU ....

D **Writing** Write a paragraph about the hotel you chose in Lesson 4. Explain why you would like to stay there. What are its advantages and disadvantages?

I would like to stay at the Hotel Casablanca.
Atmosphere is very important to me and ...

WRITING BOOSTER ▸ p. 141
- *Avoiding sentence fragments with <u>because</u> or <u>since</u>*
- *Guidance for Exercise D*

ORAL REVIEW

Pair work

1 Create a conversation between the hotel guest in Room 816 and the woman at the front desk. Ask for hotel services or complain about a problem. Start like this:

Hello? Is this the front desk?

2 Create a conversation between the man at the front desk and the caller. Use will. Complete the message slip. Start like this:

A: Front desk. Can I help you?
B: Yes, thanks. I'd like to leave a message for . . .

3 Create a conversation between the two men at the front desk. Check into or check out of the hotel. Discuss hotel amenities, services, and schedules. Start like this:

Hi. I'm checking in. The name's ....

PHONE MESSAGE

FOR: ______

FROM: ☐ Mr. ☐ Ms. ☐ Mrs. ☐ Miss ______

☐ Please call ☐ Will call again
☐ Wants to see you ☐ Returned your call

Message: ______

NOW I CAN...

- ☐ Check into a hotel.
- ☐ Leave and take a message.
- ☐ Request housekeeping services.
- ☐ Choose a hotel.

UNIT 4

Cars and Driving

Preview

GOALS After Unit 4, you will be able

1 Describe a car accident.
2 Report a problem with a car.
3 Rent a car.
4 Discuss good and bad driving.

Serving Europe and the world . . .

Maxi CARS RENTALS

Choose from the following car types:

Full-size Sedan
Daily Rate €45

Compact Car
Daily Rate €30

Wagon
Daily Rate €45

Minivan / Van
Daily Rate €55

Convertib
Daily Rate €70

SUV
Daily Rate €65

Sports Ca
Daily Rate €70

Luxury Ca
Daily Rate €80

A 2:18 **Vocabulary** • *Car types* Read and listen. Then listen again and repeat.

1 a full-size sedan	5 a convertible
2 a compact car	6 an SUV
3 a wagon	7 a sports car
4 a minivan / a van	8 a luxury car

B Discussion What factors would influence your choice of a rental car from Maxi Cars Rentals? Explain the importance of each factor.

Factors:
- daily rate
- type of car
- size of car
- pickup locations

"To me, the location of the rental office is the most important factor. If I need to rent a car, I can't get to an office that's far away!"

2:19

C 🔊 **Photo story** Read and listen to a conversation in a car rental agency.

ENGLISH FOR TODAY'S WORLD
connecting people from different cultures and language backgrounds

Renter: Good morning. The name is Kenji Kijima. I have a reservation.

Agent: Certainly, sir. Just a moment... Oh, yes. We were expecting you. A full-size sedan with GPS.

Renter: That's right.

Agent: And was that with automatic transmission or manual?

Renter: Either way.

Agent: OK, I've got a nice automatic that's all ready to go. I'll need to see your driver's license and a major credit card.

Renter: Here you go.

Agent: Thanks.

Agent: I have you returning the car on August 14th here at the airport.

Renter: Yes. That's correct.

Agent: Well, you're all set. Here are your keys and documents. The car's right outside.

Renter: Japanese speaker

D Think and explain All the following statements are false. Explain how you know they are false, using a quotation from the Photo Story.

1 The agent was surprised to see Mr. Kijima.
It's false because she says, "We were expecting you."

2 Mr. Kijima has to wait for the agency to get his car.
....

3 A passport is required at this rental agency to rent a car.
....

4 Mr. Kijima didn't choose the kind of car he wanted when he made his reservation.
....

5 Mr. Kijima can't drive a car with a manual transmission.
....

6 Mr. Kijima doesn't have his driver's license with him.
....

E Pair work Write a check mark for the situations in which it's good to rent a car. Discuss the reasons with your partner.

> "It's too expensive to rent a car for a shopping trip. It's better to ask a friend to take you."

- ☐ for a shopping trip nearby
- ☐ for travel someplace where you don't speak the language
- ☐ for a business trip with a lot of driving
- ☐ for a vacation with a large family
- ☐ for normal use when your car is in the service garage
- ☐ for another situation: ....

LESSON 1

GOAL Describe a car accident

VOCABULARY Car parts

2:20

A Read and listen. Then listen again and repeat.

EXTERIOR

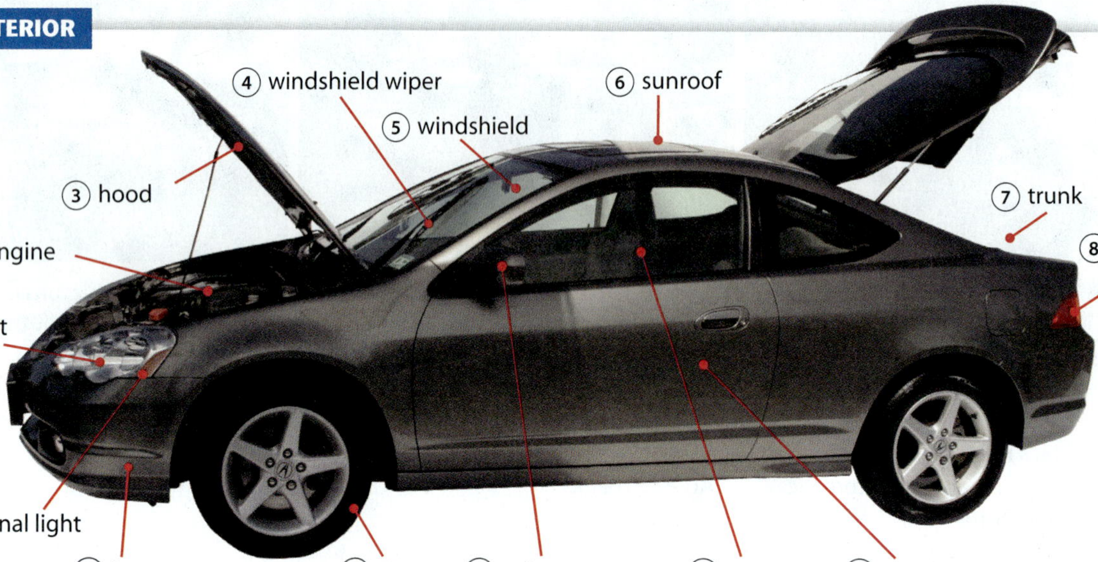

INTERIOR

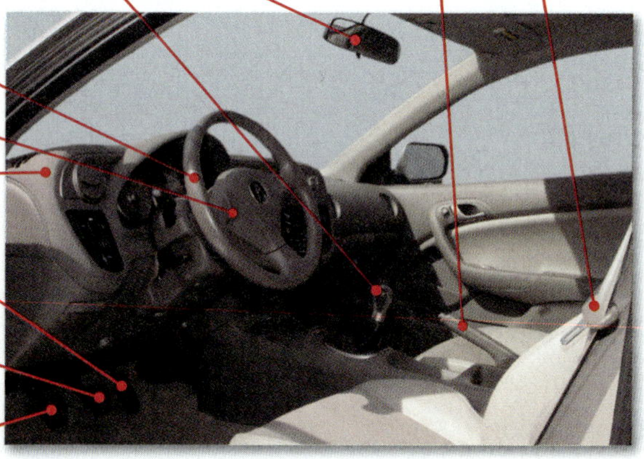

B Pair work Take turns identifying the car part for each definition.

1 a light at the back of the car
2 a light that indicates a turn
3 a part the driver uses to turn the car
4 a part that cleans the front window
5 a part that makes the car go faster
6 a part that keeps passengers safe during an accident
7 a light that helps the driver see the road
8 a place in the back for carrying things

GRAMMAR The past continuous

Use the past continuous to describe an activity that continued during a period of time in the past. Form the past continuous with was or were and a present participle.

The car **was making** a funny sound while they **were driving**.
Were the headlights **working**? (Yes, they were. / No, they weren't.)
Where **were** you **going** when it **was raining**?

Remember: The simple past tense describes a completed past action.

past continuous	simple past tense
She **was driving** home when she	**had** an accident.

GRAMMAR BOOSTER ▸ p. 127
• *The past continuous: other uses*

A Grammar practice Complete the paragraph with the past continuous or the simple past tense.

I .... (1 have) an accident yesterday. I .... (2 drive) slowly and I was sure I .... (3 pay) attention. But I .... (4 wait) for a phone call. When the phone .... (5 ring), I .... (6 answer) it. Suddenly, the car in front of me .... (7 stop), and I .... (8 hit) it. I certainly .... (9 learn) my lesson! Luckily, I .... (10 wear) a seat belt when I .... (11 have) the accident.

2:21

B Listening comprehension Listen to the conversations about accidents. Write the number of each conversation in the box under the picture.

☐

☐

☐

☐

CONVERSATION MODEL

2:22

A Read and listen to a conversation about a car accident.

A: I had an accident.

B: I'm so sorry. Are you OK?

A: I'm fine. No one was hurt.

B: Thank goodness. How did it happen?

A: Well, the other driver was tailgating, and he hit my car.

B: Oh, no! Was there much damage?

A: No. I'll only have to replace a taillight.

2:24

Ways to show concern

I'm so sorry.
Oh, no!
How awful!
I'm sorry to hear that.
That's terrible.

2:23

B Rhythm and intonation Listen again and repeat. Then practice the Conversation Model with a partner.

NOW YOU CAN Describe a car accident

Pair work Change the Conversation Model to role-play a new conversation. Describe a car accident. Use the pictures, the past continuous, and the simple past tense.

A: I had an accident.

B: .... Are you OK?

A: ....

B: .... How did it happen?

A: Well, ... , and ....

B: .... Was there much damage?

A: ....

speeding

not paying attention

talking on a cell phone

tailgating

Don't stop!
Ask about the location of the accident and other damage.

LESSON 2

GOAL Report a problem with a car

VOCABULARY *Phrasal verbs for talking about cars*

2:25

A Read and listen. Then listen again and repeat.

turn on

turn off

pick up

fill up

drop off

B Complete the sentences with the two parts of each phrasal verb.

1 The car's almost out of gas. Let's go in here so I can .... it ....
2 It's raining and I can't .... the windshield wipers .... They aren't working.
3 Do you have a van for this afternoon? I can .... it .... at 3:30.
4 We need to return the car before 6:00. Let's .... it .... early at the airport and get something to eat, OK?
5 I can't .... the air conditioning .... It's freezing in here!

GRAMMAR *Direct object placement with phrasal verbs*

Phrasal verbs contain a verb and a particle that together have their own meaning.

main verb		particle		
turn	+	on	=	start (a machine)

Many phrasal verbs are separable. This means that a direct object noun can come before or after the particle. Turn on, turn off, pick up, drop off, and fill up are separable.

I'll drop off **the car** (direct object). OR I'll drop **the car** (direct object) off.

Be careful! If the direct object is a pronoun, it must come before the particle.

I'll drop **it** off. (NOT I'll ~~drop off it~~.)
Did you fill **them** up? (NOT Did you ~~fill up them~~?)
Where will they pick **us** up? (NOT Where will they ~~pick up us~~?)

GRAMMAR BOOSTER ▸ p. 128
• *Nouns and pronouns: review*

PRONUNCIATION *Stress of particles in phrasal verbs*

2:26

A Stress changes when an object pronoun comes before the particle. Read and listen. Then listen again and repeat.

1 A: I'd like to pick up my car.
B: OK. What time can you pick it up?

2 A: They need to drop off the keys.
B: Great. When do they want to drop them off?

B Integrated practice Write statements or questions, placing the direct objects correctly. Then practice reading the sentences aloud with a partner. Use correct stress.

1 The taillights aren't working. (can't / I / on / them / turn) ....
2 They're expecting the car at 10:00. (off / drop / 10:00 / at / I'll / it) ....
3 It's too cold for air conditioning. (button / which / off / it / turns) .... ?
4 Thanks for fixing the car. (it / pick / what time / I / can / up) .... ?
5 The car is almost out of gas. (up / please / fill / it) ....

CONVERSATION MODEL

A 2:27 Read and listen to a conversation about car problems.

A: I'm dropping off my car.
B: Was everything OK?
A: Well, actually, the windshield wipers aren't working.
B: I'm sorry to hear that. Any other problems?
A: No. That's it.
B: Is the gas tank full?
A: Yes. I just filled it up.

B 2:28 **Rhythm and intonation** Listen again and repeat. Then practice the Conversation Model with a partner.

C Find the grammar Find and circle two direct objects in the Conversation Model.

NOW YOU CAN Report a problem with a car

A Notepadding Write one or more car parts for each possible car problem.

won't open / close: *the sunroof*
won't turn on / off:
(is / are) making a funny sound:
(isn't / aren't) working:

B Pair work Change the Conversation Model to role-play a new conversation. Report a problem with a car. Use your notepad for ideas. Then change partners, problems, and roles.

A: I'm dropping off my car.
B: Was everything OK?
A: Well, actually, ...
B: .... Any other problems?
A: ....

Be sure to recycle this language.

Oh, no!
I'm so sorry.
How awful!
I'm sorry to hear that.
Are you OK?
Is the car OK?
Thank goodness.
How did it happen?
Was there much damage?

C Option Role-play a conversation in which you report an accident when you drop off the car. Describe the accident. Say what you were doing when you had the accident. Use the past continuous. Then change roles. Start like this:

A: I'm dropping off my car. I had an accident ...

LESSON 3

GOAL Rent a car

BEFORE YOU LISTEN

A Discussion Review the car types on page 38. For what kind of situations would someone rent each type of car? Explain your answers.

> "A compact car is good for driving in a big city. It is easier to park in a small parking space."

B Pair work Read about each customer at a car rental agency. Choose the best type of car for each person. Discuss reasons with your partner.

1

Mr. Taylor is a businessman from Geneva, Switzerland, attending a business meeting in Kota Kinabalu, Malaysia. He doesn't have a lot of luggage. He only needs the car for local travel.

car type: ....

reason: ....

2

Ms. Peres is a banker from Porto Alegre, Brazil. Her daughter is getting married in Puebla, Mexico. She wants to drive to Puebla from Mexico City with her husband and two other children for the wedding. They have a lot of clothes and presents for the wedding.

car type: ....

reason: ....

3

Mr. Soo is a tourist from Seoul, Korea, visiting western Australia with his brother. They enjoy hiking and fishing, and they're planning a road trip through the Lake District. They plan to drive on some rough roads, so they want a car with four-wheel drive.

car type: ....

reason: ....

4

Ms. Móntez is a tourist from Veracruz, Mexico, visiting national parks and cities in the U.S. with her husband and their five children. They plan to do a lot of shopping.

car type: ....

reason: ....

5

Dr. Sato is from Osaka, Japan. He's traveling to an international medical meeting in Buenos Aires, Argentina. He has to invite three doctors to dinner and after-dinner entertainment. He likes to drive.

car type: ....

reason: ....

LISTENING COMPREHENSION

2:29

Listen to summarize Listen to the four phone conversations. Write a check if the caller rented a car. Then listen again. Write the reasons the other callers didn't rent a car.

☐ 1 ....

☐ 2 ....

☐ 3 ....

☐ 4 ....

NOW YOU CAN Rent a car

A Notepadding Plan a trip for which you need a rental car.

Destination	Pickup date	Drop off date	Number of companions	Activities

B Pair work Role-play a phone call to a car rental agency. Rent a car for the trip you planned on your notepad. Choose one of the cars from Wheels Around the World rental agency. Ask about the rate. Discuss the trip and your needs. Then change roles.

Be sure to recycle this language.

Agent
Hello. ___ Rental Agency.
How can I help you?
When will you pick up / drop off the car?
Where will you drop off the car?
Please bring your (driver's license / credit card).

Caller
I'd like to make a reservation.
I'm traveling with ___ .
It's a business trip / vacation.
I have / don't have a lot of luggage.
I'd like a (compact car).
I'd rather have a (van).
I need a car with (automatic / manual) transmission.

Wheels Around the World

Invocation SL
Daily Rate: US $60

Turbo
Daily Rate: US $90

Lexor 320i
Daily Rate: Inquire about price

Micro 220
Daily Rate: US $45

Sea Breeze
Daily Rate: US $75

Amigo
Daily Rate: US $70

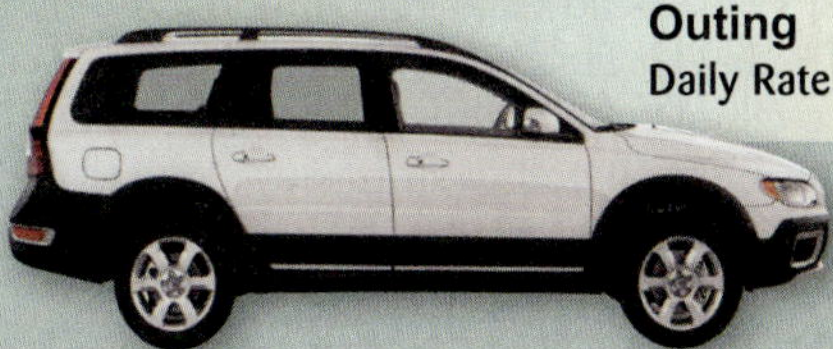

Outing
Daily Rate: US $68

Overland
Daily Rate: US $80

LESSON 4

GOAL Discuss good and bad driving

BEFORE YOU READ

A 2:30 **Vocabulary** • ***Aggressive driving behavior*** Read and listen. Then listen again and repeat.

stare

gesture

honk

flash your lights

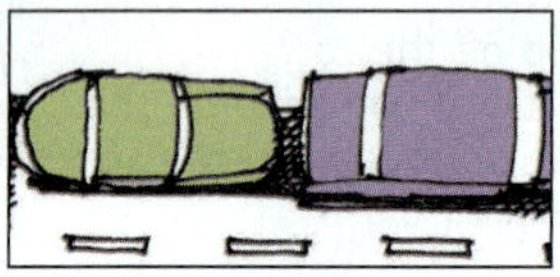

tailgate

weave through traffic

cut someone off

B Warm-up Which of the aggressive driving behaviors bother you the most? Which behaviors are the most dangerous? Why?

READING

2:31

FEATURE ARTICLE

Six Tips for Defensive Driving

We all know that not everyone drives well. Some people tailgate, gesture, weave through traffic, and honk— classic signs of the aggressive driving that causes one third of all car crashes. But more and more people are now talking on the phone, eating, and even watching TV as they drive—examples of the multitasking and inattentive driving that is a growing cause of accidents. Although we can't control the actions of other drivers, the following defensive driving tips can help us reduce the risks caused by our own driving and the bad driving of others.

1 Slow down. Driving too fast for weather or road conditions gives you less time to react to dangers on the road ahead of you. Also, as you increase your speed, your car becomes harder to control and takes longer to come to a stop.

2 Follow the "3-second rule." The greatest chance of a collision is in front of you. Maintaining a safe following distance of three seconds behind the car in front of you will give you enough time to react if that car slows or stops suddenly.

3 Pay attention to your surroundings. Be aware of where other vehicles are and what is happening on the road. Check your rearview and side-view mirrors frequently. Before changing lanes, always look over your shoulder to check your "blind spots"—areas to the side and rear of your car that aren't visible in your mirrors.

4 Signal your intentions early. Use turn signals to let other drivers know what you're going to do before you do it. This helps other drivers understand your plans, so they can make their own defensive driving decisions.

5 Expect the unexpected. Assume that other drivers will make mistakes. Plan ahead what you will do if another driver breaks a traffic law or cuts you off. For example, don't assume that a vehicle coming to a stop sign or a red light is going to stop. Be prepared to stop your own car if necessary.

6 Don't take others' aggressive driving personally. Other people will drive badly. They're not thinking about you. If you permit them to make you angry, it can affect your own driving and lead to an accident. When other drivers show signs of aggressive driving, just slow down or pull over to let them pass.

A Understand from context Circle the correct word or phrase to complete each statement.

1 A person who is doing more than one activity at the same time is (multitasking / driving defensively).
2 Following the "3-second rule" means maintaining a safe (road condition / following distance).
3 Tailgating, gesturing, and honking are three examples of (inattentive / aggressive) driving.
4 Not paying attention is an example of (inattentive / aggressive) driving.
5 *Collision* and *crash* are two words that mean (danger / accident).
6 A part of the road that you can't see in your mirrors is called a (blind spot / lane).

B Critical thinking How can defensive driving help drivers avoid accidents? Explain your opinion, using the Vocabulary and examples from the Reading or from your own experience.

On your *ActiveBook* Self-Study Disc:
Extra Reading Comprehension Questions

NOW YOU CAN Discuss good and bad driving

A Pair work Complete the survey and then compare surveys with a partner. Do the same things bother you?

How does the driving behavior of others affect you?

Rate each behavior on a scale of 1 to 3.

- ☐ Tailgating to make others go faster or get out of the way
- ☐ Making rude gestures at others
- ☐ Honking excessively
- ☐ Staring angrily at other drivers
- ☐ Flashing lights to signal others to move to another lane
- ☐ Weaving in and out of traffic
- ☐ Driving too slowly
- ☐ Cutting other drivers off

1 = Doesn't bother me
2 = Annoys me
3 = Makes me very angry

☐ **Total your score.**

If your score is...

- **20-24** Calm down. Don't take other people's bad driving personally. They're not thinking about you.
- **13-19** Stay focused. Don't allow bad drivers to distract you. Pay attention to your own driving instead.
- **8-12** Congratulations! You're as cool as a cucumber.

B Notepadding Make a list of good and bad driving behaviors.

Good drivers	Bad drivers
pay attention	flash their lights at others

C Discussion Discuss good and bad driving. Do you think most people are good drivers? Use your notepad for support.

Text-mining (optional)
Underline language in the Reading on page 46 to use in the Discussion. For example:
"If the driver of another vehicle is ..."

Review

More Practice
ActiveBook *Self-Study Disc*
grammar • vocabulary • listening
reading • speaking • pronunciation

2:32
A 🔊 **Listening comprehension** Listen to the conversations. Then complete the statements with aggressive driving behavior vocabulary from page 46.

1 The other driver just .... them ....
2 Jim's mother says he's ....
3 The driver behind them is .... at them.
4 The driver opened his window and .... at them.
5 The driver is .... because he wants to pass.
6 The driver is ....
7 The driver is .... at them.

2:33/2:34
Top Notch Pop
"Wheels around the World"
Lyrics p. 149

B Read the definition. Write the name of the car part.

1 a window on the top of the car: ....
2 a part that stops the car: ....
3 a window the driver looks through to see the cars in front: ....
4 a place where the driver can find information about speed and amount of gas: ....
5 a part that people wear to avoid injuries in an accident: ....
6 a part that prevents the car from moving when it's parked: ....

C Complete each statement or question about driving. Use the past continuous or the simple past tense.

1 I .... (not pay attention), and I .... (have) an accident.
2 The other driver .... (not stop) at the stop sign, and she .... (not wear) a seat belt.
3 He .... (talk) on a cell phone and his car .... (damage) my trunk.
4 Who .... (drive) when the accident .... (occur)?
5 Where .... they .... (stand) when they .... (see) the accident?

D Complete each conversation, putting the phrasal verbs and objects in order.

1 A: Won't the car start?
B: No, I / it / can't / turn / on ....

2 A: Do you need gas, sir?
B: Yes. Please / up / fill / it ....

3 A: Hey, you haven't turned on your headlights.
B: Oops. Thanks. I can't believe / I / forgot / turn / on / to / them ....
....

4 A: Can All Star Limo drive us to the airport?
B: Yes. They / us / pick / will / up / at 5:30 ....

E **Writing** On a separate sheet of paper, write a short paragraph about the differences between good and bad drivers.

WRITING BOOSTER ▸ p. 142
- *Connecting words and sentences:* And, In addition, Furthermore, *and* Therefore
- *Guidance for Exercise E*

ORAL REVIEW

Group story Together, create a story about the pictures. Each person adds one sentence to the story. Begin with January 16. Use the past continuous and the simple past tense in your story. Start like this:

They picked up their rental car in Temuco on January 16...

Pair work

1 Create conversations for the people in the first three pictures. For example:

A: We're here to pick up our car.
B: Certainly. Can you show me your driver's license and a credit card, please?

2 Create a phone conversation for the fourth picture. The woman reports the accident to Multi Car Rentals. The agent responds. Say as much as you can. For example:

We had an accident. My husband was...

NOW I CAN...

- ☐ Describe a car accident.
- ☐ Report a problem with a car.
- ☐ Rent a car.
- ☐ Discuss good and bad driving.

UNIT 5

Personal Care and Appearance

Preview

GOALS After Unit 5, you will be abl

1 Ask for something in a store.
2 Request salon services.
3 Discuss ways to improve appearance.
4 Define the meaning of beauty.

THE GREEN DOOR

AT THE IMPERIAL HOTEL

Unique 24-hour Unisex Spa for Hotel Guests

Relieve stress and the aches and pains of your busy, tension-filled life.

Surround yourself with the best in personal care delivered by multinational, multilingual technicians.

Massages
Relax with a Swedish or Shiatsu massage.

Manicures
Make your nails beautiful with a Russian or French manicure.

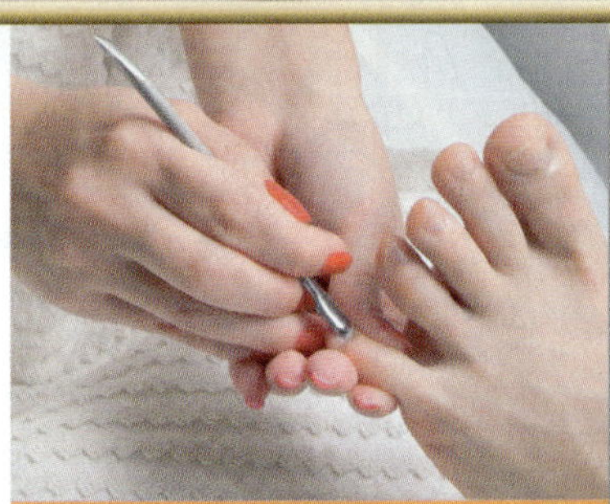

Pedicures
Get ready for sandals season! For men and women.

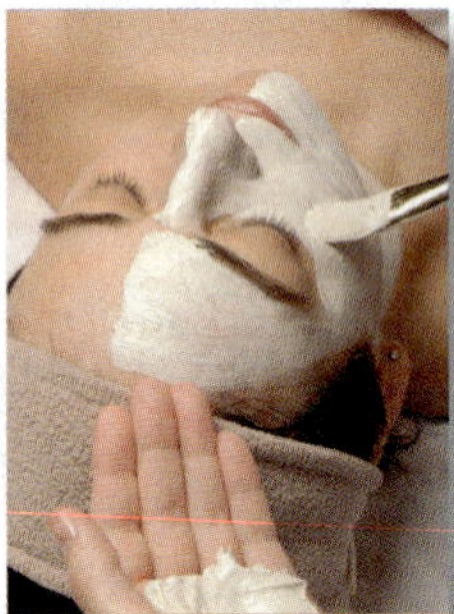

Facials
Make yourself look ten years younger!

Shaves
Let Omar and his expert staff give you the best shave in town!

Haircuts
All the latest international styles. Hair coloring and straightening available, too.

APPOINTMENTS SUGGESTED • WALK-INS WELCOME • TOUCH 6 ON YOUR ROOM PHONE

3:02

A **Vocabulary** • ***Salon services*** Read and listen. Then listen again and repeat.

a massage   a manicure   a pedicure   a facial   a shave   a haircut

B **Pair work** Take turns asking questions about the salon services.

"What salon service should you get when your hair is too long?"

3:03

C 🔊 **Photo story** Read and listen to a conversation at a hotel salon.

ENGLISH FOR TODAY'S WORLD
connecting people from different cultures and language backgrounds

Receptionist: Can I help you, sir?

Client: Would it be possible to get a massage? I don't have an appointment.

Receptionist: Well, actually, you're in luck. Our eleven o'clock just called to cancel his appointment.

Client: Terrific.

Receptionist: Let me show you to the dressing area.

Client: Thanks. Oh, while I'm at it, do you think I could get a haircut, too?

Receptionist: Yes. But you might have to wait a bit. We don't have anything until 12:00.

Client: Not a problem. By the way, how much will the massage and haircut come to? I don't have much cash on me.

Receptionist: Let's see, it will be 110 euros in all. But you can charge it to your room.

Client: Great. One more question. Is it customary to tip the staff?

Receptionist: Well, that's up to you. But most clients give the stylist and the masseuse a euro or two each.

Receptionist: French speaker

D **Focus on language** Answer the following questions, using language from the Photo Story.

1. How does the client ask for a massage?
2. How does the receptionist indicate that the client can have a massage without an appointment?
3. How does the client say "That's OK"?
4. How does the client ask about the price of a massage and a haircut?
5. What phrase does the receptionist use to tell the client the total cost of the salon services?
6. How does the receptionist tell the client that he doesn't have to pay until he checks out of the hotel?
7. What expression does the receptionist use to tell the client that the amount to tip is <u>his</u> decision?

E **Personalize** Check the word or phrase that best describes how often you get these salon services. Then compare charts with a partner.

	never	once in a while	monthly	weekly	too often to count
shampoo	☐	☐	☐	☐	☐
haircut	☐	☐	☐	☐	☐
facial	☐	☐	☐	☐	☐
shave	☐	☐	☐	☐	☐
manicure	☐	☐	☐	☐	☐
pedicure	☐	☐	☐	☐	☐
massage	☐	☐	☐	☐	☐

F **Pair work** In your opinion, what is the value of each of these services? Compare opinions with a partner.

" I think massages are great for backaches. A massage helps me feel better. "

" A shave? Are you kidding? I do that myself. I don't go to salons! "

LESSON 1

GOAL Ask for something in a store

VOCABULARY *Personal care products*

3:04

A Read and listen. Then listen again and repeat.

count nouns

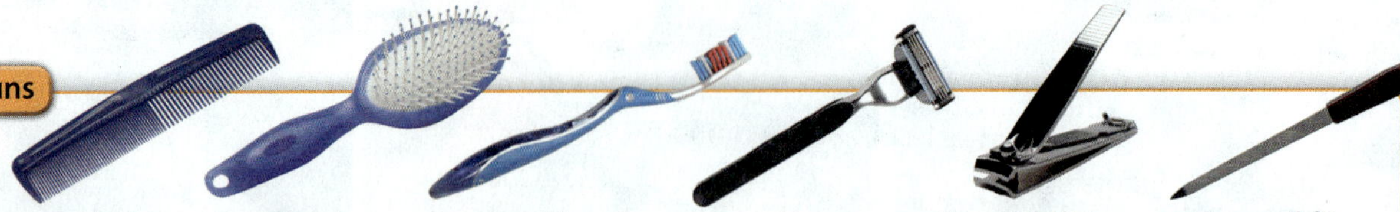

1 a comb
2 a brush
3 a toothbrush
a razor
5 a nail clipper
6 a nail file

non-count nouns

1 soap
2 deodorant
3 shaving cream
4 aftershave
5 toothpaste
6 shampoo
7 hairspray
8 sunscreen
9 dental floss
10 hand and body lotion

11 makeup

12 lipstick
mascara
eye shadow
15 face powder
16 nail polish

3:05

B **Listening comprehension** Listen and circle the kind of product each ad describes.

1 Spring Rain (shampoo / deodorant)
2 Rose (soap / nail polish)
3 Pro-Tect (sunscreen / hand and body lotion)
4 All Over (face powder / hand and body lotion)
5 Scrubbie (toothpaste / shaving cream)
6 Maximum Hold (hairspray / shampoo)

GRAMMAR *Quantifiers for indefinite quantities and amounts*

Use some and any with both plural count nouns and non-count nouns.

some: affirmative statements
We bought **some** combs. Now we have **some**.
They need **some** soap. We have **some**.

any: negative statements
I don't have **any** razors. I don't want **any**.
We don't want **any** makeup. We don't need **any**.

some or any: questions
Do you want **any** aftershave? OR Do you want **some** aftershave?
Does she have **any** nail files? OR Does she have **some** nail files?

Use a lot of with both plural count nouns and non-count nouns in statements and questions.
That store has **a lot of** razors. / They don't have **a lot of** sunscreen. / Do they have **a lot of** makeup?

Use many and much in negative statements.

many: with plural count nouns	**much: with non-count nouns**
They don't have **many** brands of makeup.	The store doesn't have **much** toothpaste.

GRAMMAR BOOSTER ▸ p. 128

- *Some and any: indefiniteness*
- *Too many, too much, and enough*
- *Comparative quantifiers fewer and less*

Grammar practice Complete the conversation between a husband and wife packing for a trip.

Dana: Do we have (1 any / many) shampoo?
Neil: Yes. We have (2 many / a lot of) shampoo.
Dana: And Maggie uses (3 much / a lot of) sunscreen. Is there (4 many / any)?
Neil: No, there isn't (5 some / any). And we don't have (6 much / many) toothpaste, either. I can pick (7 some / any) up on my way back from work.
Dana: Hey, Adam's shaving now. Does he need (8 any / much) shaving cream?
Neil: He doesn't shave every day. He can use mine!

CONVERSATION MODEL

3:06
A Read and listen to someone looking for personal care products in a store.

A: Excuse me. Where would I find sunscreen?
B: Sunscreen? Have a look in the cosmetics section, in aisle 2.
A: Actually, I did and there wasn't any.
B: I'm sorry. Let me get you some from the back. Anything else?
A: Yes. I couldn't find any razors either.
B: No problem. There are some over there. I'll show you.

3:07
B **Rhythm and intonation** Listen again and repeat. Then practice the Conversation Model with a partner.

C **Find the grammar** Find and circle all the quantifiers in the Conversation Model.

NOW YOU CAN Ask for something in a store

A **Pair work** Use the store directory to role-play a conversation. Change the Conversation Model, using other products and quantifiers. Then change roles.

A: Excuse me. Where would I find .... ?
B: .... ? Have a look in ....
A: Actually, I did and there .... any.
B: I'm sorry. Let me get you .... from the back. Anything else?
A: ....

Cosmetics Plus
DIRECTORY

	Aisle
Hair Care	3
Tooth Care	4
Skin Care	2
Nail Care	2
Makeup	2
Shaving Supplies	1

B **Change partners** Change the kind of store and ask for other kinds of products.

Other products
- clothes
- food
- electronics

GOAL Request salon services

CONVERSATION MODEL

A 3:08 Read and listen to someone request salon services.

A: I'm Linda Court. I have a two o'clock appointment for a haircut with Sean.

B: Hello, Ms. Court. Sean's running a little late. Do you mind waiting?

A: Not at all. Can I get a manicure in the meantime?

B: Yes, but it'll be a few minutes. There's someone ahead of you.

B 3:09 **Rhythm and intonation** Listen again and repeat. Then practice the Conversation Model with a partner.

GRAMMAR *Indefinite pronouns: someone / no one / anyone*

Someone, no one, and anyone are indefinite pronouns. Each refers to an unnamed person. Use indefinite pronouns when the identity of the person is unknown or unimportant.

Affirmative statements

There's {someone / no one} ahead of you.

{Someone / No one} is waiting for the manicurist.

I saw **someone** at the front desk.

Negative statements

There isn't **anyone** waiting.
I didn't see **anyone** at the salon.

Questions

Can {anyone / someone} wash my hair?

Is there {anyone / someone} at the front desk?

Did you see {anyone / someone} waiting for a shave?

Be careful!
Use anyone, not no one, with the negative form of a verb.
DON'T SAY I didn't speak to ~~no one~~.

GRAMMAR BOOSTER ▸ p. 130
• *Indefinite pronouns: something, anything, and nothing*

A 3:10 **Listening comprehension** Listen to the conversations. Complete each statement with someone or anyone and the salon service(s).

1 They can't find .... to give her a .... this afternoon.
2 .... can give him a .... and a .... at 4:00.
3 There is .... who can give her a .... and a .... at 6:30.
4 There isn't .... who can give him a .... today.

B Grammar practice Complete each statement or question with <u>someone</u>, <u>no one</u>, or <u>anyone</u>. In some cases, more than one answer is correct.

1 There's *someone* (or *no one*) at the front desk.
2 They didn't tell .... it would be a long wait.
3 Did you see .... giving a manicure?
4 I don't have the nail file. I gave it to ....
5 There will be .... here to give you a pedicure in a few minutes.
6 .... can cut your hair at 12:30 if you can wait.
7 Please don't tell .... the price. It was very expensive!
8 .... called and left you this message while you were getting your shampoo.
9 Please give this list of services to .... to read.
10 There wasn't .... there when she called for an appointment.
11 I didn't speak to .... about the bad haircut.
12 .... told me the salon offers Shiatsu massage now.
13 I didn't ask .... about the price.

PRONUNCIATION Pronunciation of unstressed vowels

A 3:11 The vowel in an unstressed syllable is often pronounced /ə/. Read and listen, paying attention to the syllable or syllables marked with /ə/. Then listen again and repeat.

1 ma ssage (ma = /ə/)
2 fa cial (cial = /ə/)
3 ma ni cure (ni = /ə/)
4 pe di cure (di = /ə/)
5 de o do rant (o = /ə/, rant = /ə/)

B Now practice saying the words on your own.

NOW YOU CAN Request salon services

A Pair work Create a conversation requesting salon services. Change the Conversation Model, using the services and staff at the Unisex Salon. Then change roles.

A: I'm .... I have .... appointment for .... with ....
B: Hello, ... running a little late. Do you mind waiting?
A: Not at all. Can I get a .... in the meantime?
B: ....

Be sure to recycle this language.

I'd like to make an appointment for a ___ on ___ .
Is someone available on ___ ?
How much do you charge for a ___ ?

Don't stop!

- Make an appointment for your next visit.
- Make an appointment for someone else.
- Change the ending.

B Change partners Make appointments for other services.

UNISEX SALON

Services	Staff
shampoo	Lisa / Choi
haircut	Judy / Jun / Bruce
manicure	Sonia / Natasha
pedicure	Karin
shave	Nick
facial	Svetlana / Ella
massage	Vladimir / Edouard

LESSON 3

GOAL Discuss ways to improve appearance

BEFORE YOU READ

Predict Look at the photos and title of the article. What questions do you think the people will ask Dr. Weiss?

READING

3:12

Write a letter to Dr. Weiss:
The Daily Mail
1601 Carroll Mews
Munyville, NY 10544

Cosmetic surgery—for everyone? Q A

Some people consider cosmetic surgery no more serious than visiting a spa or a salon. But others say, "I think I'll pass." They're aware that cosmetic surgery is, in fact, surgery, and surgery should never be taken lightly. Cosmetic surgeons have made great progress in repairing injuries and damage from burns. But more and more, people with the necessary financial resources have chosen cosmetic surgery to improve appearance. Fitness editor Dr. Gail Weiss answers readers' questions about cosmetic surgery.

Dear Dr. Weiss:
When I was young, I was a chocoholic. I ate a lot of chocolate, but I never gained any weight. Now that I'm older, I can't eat anything without gaining weight! I've heard that liposuction is the answer to an overweight person's dreams. What's up with that?

Dawson

Dear Dawson:
It's true that liposuction can remove fat deposits that don't respond to dieting and exercise, but it's expensive and can be dangerous. It would be a good idea to ask your doctor for some help in dieting first. Then, if you are unsuccessful, be sure to find a surgeon with a lot of experience before deciding on liposuction.

Gail Weiss, M.D.

Dear Dr. Weiss:
I'm a 24-year-old man who is already losing his hair. Dr. Weiss, I'm looking for a wife and I'm afraid no woman will want to marry a 25-year-old baldie! I need some advice.

Calvin

Dear Calvin:
There are several surgical procedures which a cosmetic surgeon can perform to help treat hair loss and restore hair for both men and women. But if that's not practical, remember that some of the world's most attractive men are bald!

Gail Weiss, M.D.

Dear Dr. Weiss:
Can anyone help me with my problem? I have too much hair on my body and I'm sick and tired of shaving. It's so embarrassing!

Cassandra

Dear Cassandra:
Before you call a cosmetic surgeon for hair removal, try a depilatory cream. Depilatories are available in any drugstore, and they remove hair easily and safely in your own home. Why don't you give that a try first?

Gail Weiss, M.D.

BEFORE cosmetic surgery **AFTER** cosmetic surgery

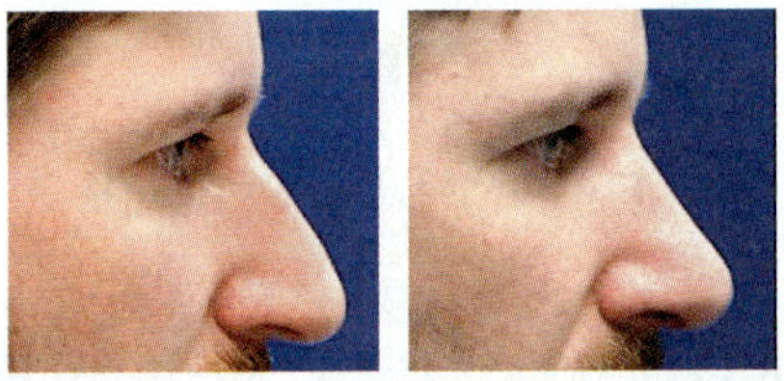

Dear Dr. Weiss:
I'm at my wits' end with my face. I have wrinkles and sun damage. I'm only 30 but I look 50. Do you think a face-lift is an option for me?

Josephine

Dear Josephine:
Both men and women of all ages request this popular and effective surgery. It lifts the face and the neck in one operation and has excellent results. But this is surgery, and afterwards you will have to stay home for a number of days. It takes time to recover. And you may have to do it again after a number of years. Before you decide to have a face-lift, ask your dermatologist or a cosmetic surgeon about a chemical peel. A chemical peel removes the top layer of skin and can improve the appearance of the skin without surgery. Compared to surgery, a half-hour visit to your dermatologist would be a piece of cake! Good luck!

Gail Weiss, M.D.

Information Source: cosmeticsurgery.org

Confirm content and apply information Complete the chart with information from the article. Then, with a partner, give your own advice for each person.

On your *ActiveBook* Self-Study Disc: **Extra Reading Comprehension Questions**

	Problem	Dr. Weiss's advice	Your advice
Dawson			
Calvin			
Cassandra			
Josephine			

NOW YOU CAN Discuss ways to improve appearance

A Frame your ideas Take the opinion survey about ways to improve appearance.

How far would you go to improve your appearance?

Would you try...	definitely	maybe	probably not	absolutely not!
diet?	○	○	○	○
exercise?	○	○	○	○
massage?	○	○	○	○
creams and lotions?	○	○	○	○
hair removal?	○	○	○	○
hair restoration?	○	○	○	○
makeup?	○	○	○	○
facials?	○	○	○	○
face-lifts?	○	○	○	○
liposuction?	○	○	○	○
chemical peels?	○	○	○	○

B Notepadding Choose one method you would try and one method you would not try. On the notepad, write advantages and disadvantages.

Method	Advantage(s)	Disadvantage(s)
I would try diet.	*free, safe*	*It's hard to do!*

Method	Advantage(s)	Disadvantage(s)

C Discussion What's the best way to improve your appearance? What ways would you NOT try? Explain. Use your notepad for support.

Text-mining (optional) Underline language in the Reading on page 56 to use in the Discussion. For example: "___ has excellent results."

LESSON 4

GOAL Define the meaning of beauty

BEFORE YOU LISTEN

3:13
A 🔊 **Vocabulary** • ***Discussing beauty*** Read and listen. Then listen again and repeat.

physical features: skin, hair, body shape and size, eyes, nose, mouth, etc.

beauty: having physical features most people of a particular culture consider good-looking

attractive: having a beautiful or pleasing physical or facial appearance

unattractive: the opposite of *attractive*

youth: the quality of being young; the opposite of *old age*

health: the general condition of one's body and how healthy one is

B **Explore your ideas** On a separate sheet of paper, describe the characteristics of an attractive woman and an attractive man.

An attractive woman has long hair and dark eyes.

C **Pair work** Talk about the physical features you consider attractive for men and women. Use the Vocabulary and your ideas from exercise B.

"In my opinion, an attractive woman has..."

LISTENING COMPREHENSION

3:14
A 🔊 **Listen to summarize** Listen to the interview. Check all of the statements that summarize Maya Prasad's and Ricardo Figueroa's ideas about beauty.

Maya Prasad

- ☐ I'm very lucky to be so beautiful.
- ☐ All the contestants were beautiful. I was just lucky.
- ☐ Physical beauty only lasts a short time.
- ☐ Love makes people beautiful.

Ricardo Figueroa

- ☐ Physical beauty is not important at all.
- ☐ Both physical beauty and inner beauty are important.
- ☐ Only inner beauty is important.
- ☐ Prasad represents an almost perfect combination of inner and outer beauty.

3:15
B 🔊 **Listen to take notes** Listen and take notes about what Figueroa says about each of the qualities below. Then compare your notes with the class.

warmth:

patience:

goodness and kindness:

C Discussion Talk about one or more of the following questions.

1 In what ways do you agree or disagree with Prasad's and Figueroa's ideas about beauty?
2 Do you think the Miss World contest sounds better than the usual beauty contest? Why or why not?
3 Do you think there should be beauty contests for men as well as for women? Why or why not? What in your opinion is the difference between a woman's beauty and a man's beauty?
4 How do you explain these words in the song Prasad talks about: "Do you love me because I'm beautiful, or am I beautiful because you love me"?

NOW YOU CAN Define the meaning of beauty

A Notepadding Look at the four photos. What qualities of beauty do you find in each person? Write notes.

1	Outer beauty	Inner beauty
	She has beautiful skin.	*She looks warm and friendly.*

1 Outer beauty

Inner beauty

2 Outer beauty

Inner beauty

3 Outer beauty

Inner beauty

4 Outer beauty

Inner beauty

B Pair work Discuss the qualities of beauty you found in the people in the pictures. Compare your opinions. Use your notepads for support.

C Discussion Define the meaning of beauty.

"I think beauty is hard to describe. It's a combination of things. I consider my grandmother really beautiful because..."

Review

More Practice
ActiveBook Self-Study Disc
grammar • vocabulary • listening
reading • speaking • pronunciation

3:16
A Listening comprehension Listen to the conversations. Infer what kind of product the people are discussing. Complete each statement.

1 Hawaii Bronzer is a brand of ....
2 Swan is a brand of ....
3 Truly You is a brand of ....
4 Mountain Fresh is a brand of ....
5 Silk 'n Satin is a brand of ....
6 Fresh as a Flower is a brand of ....

B Complete each statement or question.

1 There aren't (many / much) customers in the store right now.
2 Do they sell (any / many) sunscreen at the hotel gift shop? I forgot to pack some.
3 Your sister doesn't want (some / any) body lotion.
4 She doesn't wear (much / some) makeup. She doesn't need to—she has beautiful skin.
5 My son uses (any / a lot of) shaving cream.
6 There's (anyone / someone) on the phone for you. Do you want me to take a message?
7 There are (any / a lot of) salons in this neighborhood.

C Complete each statement about salon services.

1 There's nothing like a professional .... when you're sick and tired of your beard.
2 If your hair is too long, get a ....
3 If the skin on your face looks tired and dry, get a ....
4 In the summer, before you wear sandals for the first time, your feet will look great if you get a ....
5 When your hands are a mess, you can get a ....
6 When your muscles are sore from too much work or exercise, a .... can help.

D Complete each conversation in your own way.

1 A: Is it ....?
B: That's up to you. Most people give about 10 percent of the bill to the hair stylist.

2 A: Would you ....?
B: I think I'll pass. I don't have much cash on me.

3 A: How ....?
B: The two together will come to about US $60. But you can charge it to your room.

4 A: Can I ....?
B: Actually, you're in luck. We've just had a cancellation.

5 A: I have ....
B: Oh, yes. Welcome. Olga can see you right away.

3:17/3:18
Top Notch Pop
"Piece of Cake"
Lyrics p. 149

E Writing Re-read the letters on page 56. Choose one letter and write a response, using your own opinion and making your own suggestions. Explain what you think is OK or appropriate for men and women.

WRITING BOOSTER ▸ p. 143
- *Writing a formal letter*
- *Guidance for Exercise E*

ORAL REVIEW

Contest Look at the picture for a minute, and then close your books. With a partner, try to remember all the products and services in the picture. The pair who remembers the most products and services wins.

Pair work

1 Create a conversation between the client and the clerk at the front desk of the hotel salon. Start like this:

Hi. I have a 2:30 appointment for . . .

2 Create a conversation for the man and woman waiting for salon services. For example:

What are you here for?

NOW I CAN...

- ☐ Ask for something in a store.
- ☐ Request salon services.
- ☐ Discuss ways to improve appearance.
- ☐ Define the meaning of beauty.

TOP NOTCH
2A
Grammar Booster

Grammar Booster

The Grammar Booster is optional. It is not required for the achievement tests in the *Top Notch Complete Assessment Package.* If you use the Grammar Booster, there are additional Grammar Booster exercises in the Workbook in a separate labeled section.

UNIT 1 *Lesson 1*

The present perfect: information questions

Form information questions by inverting have and the subject of the sentence.

What **have** you **seen** in Paris?
What (OR Which) countries **have** you **visited**?
Where **has** she **found** the best souvenirs?
How **have** your parents **been**?
How many cities **have** you **visited** this week?
Who **have** you **traveled** with?

Note: When Who is the subject of the sentence, there is no inversion.
Who **has traveled** to Miami in the last two months?

On a separate sheet of paper, write information questions. Use the present perfect.

1 what dishes / she / try / in Mérida
2 who / you / invite / to the party
3 where / he / work / before
4 which movies / they / see
5 how / your children / be
6 who / climb / Grouse Mountain
7 what / they / hear / about the new school
8 how many times / she / take / that class

UNIT 1 *Lesson 2*

The present perfect: use and placement of yet and already

Use already in affirmative statements. Place already before the main verb or at the end of the statement.
I've **already** read the book. OR I've read the book **already**.

Use yet in negative statements. Place yet at the end of the statement or between have and the base form.
I haven't read the book **yet**. OR I haven't **yet** read the book.

Use yet or already in questions.
Have you read the book **yet**? OR { Have you **already** read the book? / Have you read the book **already**? }

Be careful!
Don't use yet in affirmative statements. Don't use already in negative statements.
DON'T SAY Yes, I've read the book ~~yet~~. / No, I haven't ~~already~~ read the book.
Don't use ever with yet or already.
DON'T SAY Have you ~~ever~~ read the book ~~yet~~? / Have you ~~ever~~ read the book ~~already~~?

A On a separate sheet of paper, rewrite each statement or question, using already or yet.

1 (yet) Has she finished the homework?
2 (yet) They haven't seen the movie.
3 (already) We've tried fried clams several times.
4 (already) Has your father left?

B On a separate sheet of paper, rewrite each sentence, using already or yet.

1 I haven't had dinner.
2 She's been to London, Berlin, and Rome.
3 They haven't called home.
4 We've finished our class.

The present perfect: ever, never, and before

Use ever in questions. Use never in negative statements and short answers. Do not use ever in affirmative statements.

Have you **ever** made sushi? { Yes, I have. OR Yes, I've made sushi. NOT Yes, I've ~~ever~~ made sushi.
No, I **never** have. OR No, I've **never** made sushi.

You can also use before in negative statements with never.

I've **never** been to Thailand **before**.

In very informal speech, ever is sometimes used to strongly emphasize never. This meaning of ever is similar to "in my whole life."

I've **never ever** been to Thailand.

C On a separate sheet of paper, answer each question, using real information. If the answer is yes, write when this happened.

1 Have you ever gone on a cruise?
2 Have you ever tried Indian food?
3 Have you ever been to Hawaii?
4 Have you ever met a famous person?
5 Have you ever fallen in love?
6 Have you ever played golf?

UNIT 2 *Lesson 1*

The present perfect and the present perfect continuous: unfinished actions

Unfinished (or continuous) actions are those that began in the past, continue in the present, and may possibly continue into the future. Here are three ways to talk about unfinished actions:

1 the present perfect with since: Use since with a stated start time in the past.
I've lived here **since** 2001. (2001 is the stated start time. I still live here, so the action "continues.")

2 the present perfect with for: Use for to describe the period of time from its start until the present.
I've lived here **for** five years. (Emphasis is on the five-year period. I still live here, so the action "continues.")

3 the present perfect continuous with for or since. (Form the present perfect continuous with the present perfect of be and a present participle.)
I'**ve been living here** since 2001. OR I'**ve been living here** for five years. (In both cases, the action "continues.")

When describing continuing and unfinished actions with for and since, the present perfect and the present perfect continuous are both correct. Some people feel the present perfect continuous emphasizes the continuing time a bit more.

A Read the sentences with the present perfect. Check each sentence that describes an unfinished (or continuing) action.

☐ **1** The Grants have lived in Buenos Aires since the late seventies.
☐ **2** Carmen has been living in Buenos Aires since last year.
☐ **3** I've visited Paris three times.
☐ **4** Ted has been visiting Paris since the 1980's.
☐ **5** We have eaten in that great Indian restaurant for years.
☐ **6** They've eaten in that Indian restaurant before.
☐ **7** My brother has been playing tennis for many years.
☐ **8** Min-ji has played tennis twice.

B Complete each statement with the present perfect continuous.

1 *Wall-E* ______________________ (play) at the Children's Classics Cinema every Saturday since 2009.
2 Robert ______________________ (wait) in the ticket holders' line for a pretty long time.
3 People ______________________ (worry about) violence in movies since the sixties.
4 I'______________________ (talk about) that movie for weeks.
5 We'______________________ (come) to this classics movie theater for two years.

Spelling rules for the present participle: review

Add -ing to the base form of the verb

speak → speak**ing**

If the base form ends in a silent -e, drop the -e and add -ing.

hav**e** → hav**ing**

In verbs of one syllable, if the last three letters are a consonant-vowel-consonant (C-V-C) series, double the last consonant and then add -ing.

C V C
s i t → si**t**ting

Be careful! Don't double the last consonant in words that end in -w, -x, or -y.

flow → flow**ing**
fix → fix**ing**
pay → pay**ing**

In verbs of more than one syllable that end in a consonant-vowel-consonant series, double the last consonant only if the stress is on the last syllable.

contról → contro**l**ling BUT órder → ordering

C **On a separate sheet of paper, write the present participle for the following base forms.**

1 find	**8** go	**15** come	**22** forget	**29** begin
2 be	**9** make	**16** leave	**23** eat	**30** tell
3 lose	**10** fix	**17** drive	**24** pay	**31** bring
4 put	**11** know	**18** meet	**25** stand	**32** take
5 get	**12** speak	**19** blow	**26** think	
6 say	**13** hear	**20** give	**27** buy	
7 write	**14** let	**21** run	**28** see	

UNIT 2 *Lesson 2*

Ways to express preferences: review

Use like, prefer, or would rather with a direct object to indicate preferences. The direct object can be a noun or noun phrase, a base form, or an infinitive, depending on the structure you use.

Nouns or noun phrases

She'd like **tea**.
We'd like **an early breakfast** tomorrow.
Sarah prefers **coffee**.
Would they prefer **a horror film**?

Base forms

They'd rather **see** a comedy.
Would you rather **have** coffee or tea?
I'd rather **not go out** tonight.

Infinitives

I'd like **to go** to the movies tonight.
I prefer (OR I'd prefer) **to see** something less bloody.
She'd prefer **not to show** her children that film.

A **On a separate sheet of paper, write sentences and questions using the following words and phrases.**

1 They / prefer / see / the Woody Allen film.
2 What time / you / would rather / meet?
3 Who / would like / order / eggs for breakfast?
4 they / would rather / watch TV or go out?
5 Jason / would like / have / a large container of popcorn.
6 I'd prefer / rent / a sci-fi film tonight.
7 Her parents / would rather not / watch / anything too violent.
8 Who'd prefer / not see / that silly animated film?

B On a separate sheet of paper, answer each question in a complete sentence, expressing your own preference.

1 What genre of movie do you usually prefer?
2 What would you like to have for dinner tonight?
3 Would you rather see a comedy or a horror film?
4 Would you prefer popcorn or potato chips from the refreshment stand?
5 Would you like to rent a DVD or go out to the movies?

UNIT 3 *Lesson 1*

Expressing obligation with have to and must

Use have to and must plus a base form to express obligation when there is no other choice of action available.

Students **must take** this exam.
You **have to take** the 6:00 train if you want to arrive on time.
She **has to make** a reservation before July 15th.

Be careful!
The negative form must not expresses prohibition, not obligation.

You **must not smoke** in your room. = Don't smoke there.

The negative forms don't have to and doesn't have to express a lack of obligation.

You **don't have to show** your passport. = It isn't necessary.

Note: Must is very formal and not very common in speaking. It is generally used by a person in authority (e.g. a teacher or boss) to state policy or law. Have to is much more common in both speaking and writing. The more informal have got to* is also common in spoken English.

Sorry. **I've got to hurry**. I'm going to be late.

*There is no negative form of have got to in American English. Use don't have to or doesn't have to.

A On a separate sheet of paper, write each of the following sentences two ways: with must and with have to.

1 Hotel guests / leave / their luggage at the front desk.
2 Hotel employees / arrive / before 9:00 A.M.
3 Hotel maids / close / the door / while cleaning a room.
4 Hotel guests / park / their cars in front of the hotel.

B On a separate sheet of paper, write each of the sentences in Exercise A again, using must not to express a prohibition. Make changes so the sentence makes sense.

Hotel guests must not leave their luggage at the front desk.

C On a separate sheet of paper, write each of the sentences in Exercise A again, using don't or doesn't have to to express a lack of obligation. Make changes so the sentence makes sense.

Hotel employees don't have to arrive before 9:00 A.M.

Suggestions and advice: could, should, ought to, and had better

Use could plus a base form to suggest or ask about an alternative. There is no negative form.

They **could stay** at the Fiesta Hotel if the Milton is full.

Could they **stay** at the Fiesta Hotel if the Milton is full?

Use should or ought to plus a base form to state an opinion or give advice.

You **should** (or **ought to**) stay at the Milton. It's close to town and very cheap.

You **shouldn't stay** at the Fairway Inn. It's too expensive.

Use had better to state an opinion or give advice. The meaning is similar to should and ought to, but had better expresses the idea that there is a consequence for not doing something.

You**'d better stay** at the Milton. The other hotels are too far from town.

You**'d better not stay** at the Fairway Inn if you want to save money.

Note: In American English it's very uncommon to use ought to in the negative. It's unusual to say: You ~~ought not stay~~ at the Fairway Inn.

Ought to has the same meaning as should, but should is slightly less formal.

Don't use ought to in questions or negative statements. Use should or shouldn't instead.

D On a separate sheet of paper, write five suggestions to a visitor to your city or country, using could, should, shouldn't, had better, and had better not.

You should stay at a hotel on the beach. The beaches are really beautiful, and the location is convenient.

Expectation: be supposed to

Use be supposed to to mean that someone expects an action from another person.

We**'re supposed to check out** of our room by twelve.

(The hotel expects guests to check out at that time.)

The negative form is be not supposed to.

Hotel guests **are not supposed to take** anything from their rooms.

E On a separate sheet of paper, write five sentences that describe actions your school expects from its students. Use be supposed to.

Students are supposed to come on time to class. They're not supposed to be late.

F Choose the sentence closer in meaning to each numbered statement or question.

1 Do you think the Milton Hotel is a good place to stay?

a Do you think I should stay at the Milton Hotel?

b Do you think I have to stay at the Milton Hotel?

2 If you don't have your luggage ticket, the bellman won't give you your luggage.

a You could give the bellman the ticket.

b You must give the bellman the ticket.

3 They don't accept credit cards in this hotel. They only accept cash.

a You have to pay with cash.

b You'd better pay with cash.

4 When I made the reservation, I asked for a suite.

a They could give me a suite.

b They're supposed to give me a suite.

5 Don't wear shorts in the restaurant.

a You must not wear shorts in the restaurant.

b You don't have to wear shorts in the restaurant.

UNIT 3 *Lesson 2*

Will and be going to

Use will or be going to for predictions about the future. The meaning is the same.

It'**ll rain** tomorrow.

It'**s going to rain** tomorrow.

Use be going to when you already have a plan for the future.

A: Are you coming to class tomorrow?

B: No, I'**m going to go** to the beach instead. NOT No, ~~I'll go~~ to the beach instead.

Other uses of will

Use will to talk about the immediate future when you do not already have a plan.

Maybe I'll go to the beach this weekend. NOT Maybe ~~I'm going to go~~ to the beach this weekend.

Use will to show willingness.

I'**ll eat** chicken, but **I won't eat** seafood. (expresses willingness)

Compare will with be going to:

I'**m going to eat** chicken, but I'**m not going to eat** seafood. (expresses a plan)

A On a separate sheet of paper, write five sentences about your plans for the weekend, using be going to.

B On a separate sheet of paper, write five sentences with will or won't for willingness on one of the following topics.

Topics
kinds of exercise you're willing (or not willing) to do
kinds of food you're willing (or not willing) to eat for breakfast
kinds of clothes you're willing (or not willing) to wear

UNIT 4 *Lesson 1*

The past continuous: other uses

The past continuous describes an action that was continuous until (and possibly after) the moment at which another action took place. The words when or while are often used in sentences that contrast continuing and completed actions.

He **was talking** on the phone when the storm **began**. (continuous action, then completed action)

While I **was living** in Chile, I **got married**. (continuous action, then completed action)

The past continuous also describes two continuing actions occurring in the same period of time.

While she **was driving**, her husband **was reading** the newspaper.

They **were eating**, and the music **was playing**.

On a separate sheet of paper, use the prompts to write logical sentences. Use the past continuous and the simple past in each sentence.

1 She / take a test at school / when / she / hear the fire alarm
2 While I / talk to my mother on the phone / the TV show / start
3 Mr. Park / cook dinner / when / Mrs. Park / finish the laundry
4 Mr. Kemp / work in the garden / when / the rain / begin
5 While / Claudia / pick up / their rental car / Alex / call / their hotel
6 While / Nancy / shop at the grocery store / she / see / an old friend

Nouns and pronouns: review

A noun is a word that names a person, a place, or a thing. Nouns are either common or proper. A proper noun is capitalized.

common nouns: car, windshield, doctor, woman, father
proper nouns: **M**artin, **C**aracas, **C**arla's **R**estaurant

Two functions of nouns in sentences are subjects and direct objects. The subject performs the action of the verb. The object receives the action.

subject — direct object
Carla's Restaurant serves **breakfast** all day long.

A pronoun is a word that represents or replaces a noun. Pronouns also function as subjects and direct objects.

subject pronouns: I, you, he, she, it, we, they
object pronouns: me, you, him, her, it, us, them

subject — direct object
My parents / **They** drove **the car** / **it** to the airport.

First, underline the subjects and circle the objects in the following sentences. Then label each noun either "common" or "proper." Finally, write a checkmark above each pronoun. (Note: Not every sentence contains a pronoun.)

proper — common
Italians drive fast (cars.)

1 We love big vans.
2 The children broke the side-view mirror.
3 Ms. Workman picked up the car this morning.
4 Rand loves sports cars, and his wife loves them, too.
5 A man driving a sports car hit our minivan.
6 I returned the rental car at the airport.
7 A-1 Rental Agency called me about the reservation.

UNIT 5 Lesson 1

Some and any: review

Some and any are indefinite quantifiers. They indicate an indefinite number or amount.

There are **some** toothbrushes in aisle 2. (We don't know how many.)
They are buying **some** shaving cream. (We don't know how much.)
Could I get **some** nail files? (We're not asking for a specific number of nail files.)
Do they have **any** makeup in this store? (We're not asking specifically how much.)

Be careful to use some and any correctly with count and non-count nouns:

Some: with non-count nouns and plural count nouns in affirmative statements

non-count noun — plural count noun
We need **some sunscreen** and **some combs**. They have **some** here.

Any: with non-count nouns and plural count nouns in negative statements

non-count noun — plural count noun
A: She doesn't want **any shampoo**, and he doesn't need **any nail clippers**.
B: Good! We don't have to buy **any**, then. I'm out of cash.

Any or some: with count and non-count nouns in questions

Do they need **any toothpaste** or **sunscreen** for the trip?
Do we need **any razors** or **toothbrushes**?

Remember: Count nouns name things you can count individually. They have singular and plural forms (1 nail file, 3 combs). Non-count nouns name things you cannot count individually. They don't have plural forms. Use containers, quantifiers, and other modifiers to make non-count nouns countable.

a bottle of shampoo / aftershave
a jar of face cream / deodorant
a tube of toothpaste / lipstick
a bar of soap
a can of hairspray / deodorant / shaving cream
250 milliliters of sunscreen

A On a separate sheet of paper, change the following sentences from affirmative to negative. Follow the example.

There is some shampoo in the shower. *There isn't any shampoo in the shower.*

1 There are some razors next to the sink.
2 We have some nail clippers.
3 They need some brushes for the children.
4 She's buying some mascara.
5 The salon needs some nail polish for the manicurists.
6 I want some sunscreen on my back.
7 There is some dental floss in aisle 4.
8 They need some deodorant for the trip.

B Complete each sentence with some or any.

1 I don't need _______ more hand lotion.
2 There isn't _______ makeup in the bag.
3 We don't see _______ scissors in the whole store.
4 They need _______ soap to wash their hands.
5 It's too bad that there isn't _______ toothpaste.
6 I don't see _______ combs or brushes on those shelves.
7 I know I had _______ nail files in my bag. Now I can't find them.

Too many, too much, and enough

The word too indicates a quantity that is excessive—more than someone wants or needs. Use enough to indicate that something is satisfactory.

Use too many and not too many for count nouns.
There are **too many customers** waiting in line.

Use too much and not too much for non-count nouns.
There's **too much toothpaste** on the toothbrush.

Use enough and not enough for both count and non-count nouns.
There's **enough shampoo**, but there are**n't enough razors**.

C Complete each sentence with too many, too much, or enough.

1 Let's do our nails. Do we have ___________ nail polish for both of us?
2 This shampoo has ___________ perfume. It smells awful!
3 It's not a good idea to buy ___________ fruit. We're not going to be home for a few days.
4 This menu has ___________ choices. I can't make up my mind.
5 Check the bathroom shelf to see if we have ___________ soap. Mom and Dad are coming to visit.
6 I don't like when there are ___________ brands. I can't decide which one to buy.
7 There's no way to get a haircut today. ___________ people had the same idea!
8 They don't want to spend ___________ money on makeup. They're trying to save money.

Comparative quantifiers fewer and less

Use fewer for count nouns. Use less for non-count nouns.
The Cosmetique store has **fewer brands** of makeup than the Emporium.
There's **less hand lotion** in this jar than in that bottle.

D Complete each sentence with fewer or less.

1 Which class has _______ students—the early class or the late one?
2 The recipe calls for _______ cheese than I thought.
3 It has _______ ingredients, too.
4 Don't rent from Cars Plus. They have _______ kinds of cars than International.
5 The Cineplus has _______ movies this weekend than usual.
6 Is there _______ shampoo in the large size or the economy size?

Indefinite pronouns: something, anything, and nothing

Use something in affirmative statements.
There's **something** in this box.
Use anything in negative statements.
There isn't **anything** in the fridge.
Use something or anything in yes / no questions.
Is there **something** we should talk about? Is **anything** wrong?
Nothing is the equivalent of not anything. Don't use nothing in negative statements.
There isn't **anything** in the fridge = There's **nothing** in the fridge. NOT There ~~isn't nothing~~ in the fridge.

Choose the correct indefinite pronoun to complete each sentence.

1 I need to go to the store to buy (something / anything).
2 There is (something / anything) I can do to help.
3 There isn't (something / anything) you can do to make yourself taller.
4 I went on the Internet to find (something / anything) about how to use sunscreen.
5 They have (something / anything) that helps you lose weight.
6 There's (anything / nothing) that can make you look young again.
7 They can't get (anything / nothing) to eat there after ten o'clock.

TOP NOTCH
2A
Writing Booster

Writing Booster

The Writing Booster is optional. It is intended to teach students the conventions of written English. Each unit's Writing Booster is focused both on a skill and its application to the Writing topic from the Unit Review page.

UNIT 1 *Avoiding run-on sentences*

An independent clause is a sentence with a subject and a verb.

subject	verb	
I	saw	a photo of the mountain.
It	looked	very high.

In writing, a run-on sentence is when we forget to use a coordinating conjunction, such as <u>and</u> or <u>but</u>, to combine independent clauses.

Run-on sentence ✗ ~~I saw a photo of the mountain it looked very high.~~

Correct a run-on sentence by (a) using a period to separate it into two sentences, or (b) using a coordinating conjunction to combine the two independent clauses. A comma before the conjunction is optional.

✓ I saw a photo of the mountain. It looked very high.
✓ I saw a photo of the mountain, and it looked very high.

Be careful! Do not use a comma to combine independent clauses. Use a period to separate them.

Run-on sentence ✗ ~~A new student arrived yesterday, he is from Santos.~~
✓ A new student arrived yesterday. He is from Santos.

Remember: A sentence …
- begins with a capital letter and ends with a period.
- has a subject and a verb.
- expresses a complete idea.

A Write ✗ if the item contains a run-on sentence. Write ✓ if the item is written correctly.

☐ **1** Ann is Canadian she doesn't speak French.
☐ **2** They're good students they work very hard.
☐ **3** My brother is a lawyer, he lives in Hong Kong.
☐ **4** Victor and Lisa came home late last night. They stayed up until 4:00 A.M.
☐ **5** Some people think cities are beautiful I don't agree.
☐ **6** I have been to three foreign countries, I have never been to the United States.
☐ **7** We haven't tried Polish food, but we have tried Hungarian food.
☐ **8** I have never been to the top of the Empire State Building in New York, I have been to the top of Taipei 101 in Taipei.
☐ **9** I visited Jeju in Korea and it was really beautiful.

B On a separate sheet of paper, write each of the run-on sentences in Exercise A correctly.

C Guidance for Writing (page 12) After you write about your experience in Exercise D, check carefully to see if you have written any run-on sentences. Use a period to separate the independent clauses or use the coordinating conjunctions <u>and</u> or <u>but</u> to combine them.

A paragraph is a group of sentences that relate to a topic or a theme. When your writing contains sections about a variety of topics, it is a good idea to divide it into separate paragraphs.

When there is more than one paragraph, it is customary, though not required, to include **a topic sentence** in each paragraph that summarizes or announces the main idea of the paragraph. The other sentences in the paragraph traditionally include details or facts that support the main idea. Using topic sentences makes paragraphs clearer and easier to understand.

In the writing model to the right there are two paragraphs, each beginning with a topic sentence (highlighted in yellow):

In the first paragraph, the topic sentence informs us that the paragraph will contain details about violence in movies "before the 1960s."

In the second paragraph, the topic sentence informs us that the paragraph will shift focus. The word "Today" lets the reader know what the focus of the paragraph will be.

Without the topic sentences, the ideas would run together and be difficult to follow.

Remember: Indent the first word of each new paragraph so readers know that a new section of the writing is beginning.

Before the 1960s, most movies did not show much graphic violence. When fighting or shooting occurred on the screen, it was clean: Bang! You're dead! The victim fell to the ground and died, perhaps after speaking a few final words. The viewer never saw blood or suffering. But in the late 60s, filmmakers such as Arthur Penn and Sam Peckinpah began making movies with more graphic violence, such as *Bonnie and Clyde* and *The Wild Bunch*. They believed that if audiences could see how truly horrible real violence was, people would be less violent in their own lives.

Today, special-effects technology has made it possible to create very realistic images of bloodshed and violence. Steven Prince, author of *Savage Cinema: Sam Peckinpah and the Rise of Ultraviolent Movies*, describes the difference between early movies and the movies of today: "... filmmakers can create any image that they can dream up." So, Prince believes, because of technology, movies today are more and more violent and bloody.

A Choose a topic sentence for each of the following paragraphs.

1

Some people are worried that viewing a lot of violence in movies and video games can be dangerous. They feel that it can make violence seem normal and can cause people to imitate the violent behavior, doing the same thing themselves. Other people disagree. They believe that showing violence is honest and can even be helpful.

a Many people say violence in movies can be harmful.
b People have different opinions about how violence can affect viewers.
c People imitate violent behavior they see in movies.

2

The 1967 Arthur Penn movie is about a real gang of violent bank robbers who terrorized the U.S. Southwest in the 1930s. Bonnie (Faye Dunaway) and Clyde (Warren Beatty), and their gang were believed to be responsible for thirteen deaths and many robberies before they were finally killed.

a *Bonnie and Clyde* is based on a true story.
b Arthur Penn is one of the most famous directors of the 1960s.
c There were a lot of bank robberies in the 1930s.

3

The U.S. documentary *Spellbound* visits the homes of eight finalists for the National Spelling Bee and then follows them to the finals in Washington. We get to know the kids and their families.

a Spelling bees are popular in the U.S., and there have been a number of them in Washington.
b The finals of the National Spelling Bee take place in Washington.
c Some documentaries give us an intimate view of people and their lives.

B On a separate sheet of paper, write two paragraphs of three to five sentences each with details about the following topics. Then make sure you have included a topic sentence for each paragraph that summarizes or announces the main idea of the paragraph.

Paragraph 1	**Paragraph 2**
The story of a time you (or someone else) were late to meet someone for an event	The story of what you (or the others) did after the event

C **Guidance for Writing (page 24)** On the notepad, write notes about why some people think watching violence is harmful and why others think it isn't. Use your notes as a guide for your paragraphs about violence in Exercise D. Include a topic sentence for each paragraph to summarize the main ideas.

Harmful:

Not harmful:

UNIT 3 *Avoiding sentence fragments with because or since*

Remember: You can use the subordinating conjunctions because or since to give a reason. Because and since answer the Why question. A clause that begins with because or since is called a dependent clause. A dependent clause gives information about an independent clause.

independent clause	dependent clause
I prefer the Hotel Casablanca	**because** (or **since**) it looks very interesting.

A dependent clause with because or since can also come at the beginning of a sentence. If it comes first, use a comma.

Because it looks very interesting, I prefer the Hotel Casablanca.

In writing, a dependent clause alone is an error called a "sentence fragment." It is not a sentence because it does not express a complete idea. Avoid writing sentence fragments.

Sentence fragment ✘ I prefer the Hotel Casablanca. ~~Because it looks very interesting~~.

To correct a sentence fragment with because or since, make sure it is combined with an independent clause. Or rewrite the sentence without because or since to create an independent clause.

✓ I prefer the Hotel Casablanca because it looks very interesting.

✓ I prefer the Hotel Casablanca. It looks very interesting.

A In the following paragraph, underline four sentence fragments with because or since.

When I was a child, I had three very important dreams. Because I was young, I thought they would all come true. The first one was that I wanted to be an architect. Because I loved modern buildings. Since I wanted to help people. The second dream was to be a doctor. The last one was to be a flight attendant. Since I liked to travel. Only one of my dreams became a reality. I am an architect today. Because I really love my job. I think it was really the right choice for me.

B On a separate sheet of paper, write the paragraph again. Correct all the sentence fragments. Combine the dependent clauses with independent clauses to make complete sentences.

C **Guidance for Writing (page 36)** In your paragraph about a hotel in Exercise D, include at least three reasons using because or since. Then check carefully to make sure that there are no sentence fragments.

And

And connects two or more words in a series. Use commas to separate words when there are more than two in the series. (The last comma is optional.)

I'm concerned about **aggressive and inattentive** driving. (no comma: and connects two adjectives.)

Inattentive drivers sometimes **eat and talk** on their cell phones while they are driving. (no comma: and connects two verbs of the same subject.)

Gesturing, **staring**, **and multitasking** are three things aggressive drivers often do. (A comma is necessary: and connects more than two words in a series. The comma after staring is optional.)

And can also combine two separate complete sentences into one sentence. In the new sentence, the two original sentences are called "independent clauses." The comma is common but optional.

—— complete sentence —— —— complete sentence ——

Aggressive drivers do many dangerous things. They cause a lot of crashes.

—— independent clause —— —— independent clause ——

Aggressive drivers do many dangerous things, **and** they cause a lot of crashes.

A Insert commas where necessary or optional in the following sentences.

1 She enjoys swimming hiking and fishing.

2 I don't like SUVs and other large cars.

3 We're traveling to France Italy and Spain.

4 Marianne and Sally are coming with us.

5 I'm renting a car and I'm driving it to Chicago.

6 This agency has nice convertibles vans and sports cars.

B On a separate sheet of paper, combine each pair of sentences into one sentence consisting of two independent clauses. Use and.

1 They made a call to a car rental company. They reserved a minivan for the weekend.

2 The left front headlight is broken. It won't turn on.

3 We rented a full-size sedan with a sunroof. We opened it because the weather was beautiful.

4 I hit the car in front of me. A passenger in the back seat was hurt.

5 You can drop the car off at nine o'clock. You can pick it up in the late afternoon.

In addition, Furthermore, and Therefore

Use In addition and Furthermore to add to the ideas in a previous sentence. In addition and Furthermore are approximately equal in meaning, but Furthermore is a little more formal. You can use both in the same writing to avoid a repetitive style.

People should pay attention to their own driving. **In addition**, they should be aware of the driving of others.

I think defensive driving makes sense. **Furthermore**, it has been proven to reduce the number of accidents.

Therefore introduces a result.

—— result ——

Ron has had a lot of accidents. **Therefore**, the rental company said he couldn't rent one of their cars.

Note: It's customary to use a comma after In addition, Furthermore, and Therefore.

C Complete the statements with In addition or Therefore.

1 The other driver was speeding. __________, she wasn't paying attention.

2 No one was hurt. __________, we didn't have to go to the hospital after the crash.

3 I was taking a business trip with a lot of equipment. __________, I rented a car with a lot of trunk space.

4 They need to rent a minivan for their trip to Montreal. __________, they have to stay in a pet-friendly hotel because they plan to bring their pet dog.

D **Guidance for Writing (page 48)** **In your paragraph about good and bad drivers in Exercise E, use And, In addition, Furthermore, and Therefore. Then check your paragraph carefully to see if you have used commas to separate words correctly.**

E-mails and handwritten social notes are informal ways to communicate with others. They don't have many rules. Formal letters, such as business letters, are generally typed and have conventions and rules. For these, be sure to include the following elements:

- your address
- the recipient's name (and / or position) and address
- the date of the letter
- a salutation
- a complimentary close
- your typewritten name and your handwritten signature

Note: If you know the recipient's name, the salutation should use the following format: Dear [title + last name]. It's common in a formal letter to use a colon (:) after the name. In less formal letters, a comma is appropriate.

Dear Mr. Smith:
Dear Marie,

If you don't know the recipient's name or gender, use this format:

Dear Sir or Madam: OR
To whom it may concern:

Follow the layout and punctuation in the writing model to the right.

657 Boulevard East
New Compton, Fortunia } **your address**

December 14, 2012 } **date**

Manager
The Tipton Spa
Tipton Hotel
2200 Byway
Sylvania, Sorrento } **recipient's address**

Dear Sir or Madam: } **salutation**

I'm writing to tell you that I was very happy with the service provided by the staff of the Tipton Spa when I was in Sylvania last week. The hair stylist gave me a wonderful haircut and the masseur was really top notch. I particularly enjoyed the relaxing music that played over the public address system. Finally, the prices were fair, and I left the spa feeling great.

I want you to know that I am recommending the Tipton Spa to all my friends and have told them that they should visit you even if they are staying in another hotel or if they are in Sylvania for the day. In fact, I have told them that it's worth traveling to Sylvania just to visit the spa. Congratulations on such a wonderful spa.

Sincerely, } **complimentary close**

Francine Classon } **signature**

Francine Classon } **typewritten name**

Other common complimentary closes
Cordially,
Sincerely yours,
Best regards,

A **Think of a business such as a hotel, a store, a salon, a gym, or a restaurant where you have received good service. On the notepad, write notes about the business.**

Name of business:

Address:

Why you are happy with the service:

B **On a separate sheet of paper, write a letter of thanks to the manager of the business in Exercise A. Explain what you like about the service. Use your notes and the writing model above as a guide.**

C **Guidance for Writing (page 60)** **Using the letter from page 56 that you chose, list three methods on the notepad below which a person could use to improve his or her appearance. Make notes of the advantages and disadvantages of each method. Then use your notes as a guide to help you write your response letter in Exercise E. Be sure to include your name and address, the date, a salutation, and a complimentary close in your letter.**

	Method	Advantages	Disadvantages
1.			
2.			
3.			

Top Notch Pop Lyrics

1:15/1:16

Greetings and Small Talk [Unit 1]

You look so familiar. Have we met before?
I don't think you're from around here.
It might have been two weeks ago, but I'm not sure.
Has it been a month or a year?
I have a funny feeling that I've met you twice.
That's what they call déjà vu.
You were saying something friendly, trying to be nice—and now you're being friendly, too.
One look, one word.
It's the friendliest sound that I've ever heard.
Thanks for your greeting.
I'm glad this meeting occurred.

(CHORUS)
Greetings and small talk
make the world go round.
On every winding road I've walked,
this is what I've found.

Have you written any letters to your friends back home?
Have you had a chance to do that?
Have you spoken to your family on the telephone?
Have you taken time for a chat?
Bow down, shake hands.
Do whatever you do in your native land.
I'll be happy to greet you
in any way that you understand.

(CHORUS)

Have you seen the latest movie out of Hollywood?
Have you read about it yet?
If you haven't eaten dinner, are you in the mood for a meal you won't forget?
Bow down, shake hands.
Do whatever you do in your native land.
I'll be happy to greet you
in any way that you understand.

(CHORUS)

1:33/1:34

Better Late Than Never [Unit 2]

Where have you been? I've waited for you.
I'd rather not say how long.
The movie began one hour ago.
How did you get the time all wrong?
Well, I got stuck in traffic, and when I arrived
I couldn't find a parking place.
Did you buy the tickets? You're kidding—
for real?
Let me pay you back, in that case.

(CHORUS)
Sorry I'm late.
I know you've waited here forever.
How long has it been?
It's always better late than never.

When that kind of movie comes to the big screen,
it always attracts a crowd,
and I've always wanted to see it with you—
but it looks like we've missed it now.
I know what you're saying, but actually,
I would rather watch a video.
So why don't we rent it and bring it back home?
Let's get in the car and go.

(CHORUS)

Didn't you mention, when we made our plans, that you've seen this movie recently?
It sounds so dramatic, and I'm so upset,
I'd rather see a comedy!
Well, which comedy do you recommend?
It really doesn't matter to me.
I still haven't seen 'The World and a Day'.
I've heard that one is pretty funny.

(CHORUS)

2:16/2:17

Checking Out [Unit 3]

Ms. Jones travels all alone.
She doesn't need much space—
a single room with a nice twin bed
and a place for her suitcase.
Her stay is always satisfactory,
but in the morning she's going to be checking out.
Mr. Moon will be leaving soon,
and when he does I'll say,
"Thank you, sir, for staying with us.
How do you want to pay?"
And in the end it isn't hard.
He'll put it on his credit card. He's checking out.
Would you like to leave a message?
Could you call back later?
Do you need some extra towels
or today's newspaper?
Can I get you anything?
Would you like room service?
I'm so sorry.
Am I making you nervous?
Good evening.
I'll ring that room for you.
Is that all?
I'll be glad to put you through.
I'm sorry, but he's not answering.
The phone just rings and rings.
The couple in room 586
have made a king-size mess.
Pick up the laundry. Turn down the beds.
We have another guest
coming with his family.
You'd better hurry or they will be checking out. . .

2:33/2:34

Wheels around the World [Unit 4]

Was I going too fast
or a little too slow?
I was looking out the window,
and I just don't know.
I must have turned the steering wheel
a little too far
when I drove into the bumper
of that luxury car.
Oh no!
How awful!
What a terrible day!
I'm sorry to hear that.
Are you OK?

(CHORUS)
Wheels around the World
are waiting here with your car.
Pick it up.
Turn it on.
Play the radio.
Wheels around the World—
"helping you to go far."
You can drive anywhere.
Buckle up and go.

Did I hit the red sedan,
or did it hit me?
I was talking on the cell phone
in my SUV.
Nothing was broken,
and no one was hurt,
but I did spill some coffee
on my favorite shirt.
Oh no!
Thank goodness you're still alive!
I'm so happy that
you survived.

(CHORUS)

What were you doing when you hit that tree?
I was racing down the mountain, and the brakes failed me.
How did it happen? Was the road still wet?
Well, there might have been a danger sign,
But I forget.
The hood popped open and the door fell off.
The headlights blinked and the engine coughed.
The side-view mirror had a terrible crack.
The gearshift broke. Can I bring the car back?
Oh no!
Thank goodness
you're still alive!
I'm so happy that
you survived.

(CHORUS)

3:17/3:18

Piece of Cake [Unit 5]

I need to pick up a few things
on the way back to school.
Feel like stopping at a store with me?
I'd like to, but I think I'll pass.
I don't have time today.
It's already nearly a quarter to three.

(CHORUS)
Don't worry. We'll be fine.
How long can it take?
It's easy. It'll be a piece of cake.

I need a tube of toothpaste and
a bar of Luvly soap,
some sunscreen, and a bottle of shampoo.
Where would I find makeup?
How about a comb?
Have a look in aisle one or two.

(CHORUS)

I have an appointment
for a haircut at The Spa.
On second thought, they're always running late.
My class starts in an hour.
I'll never make it now.
How long do you think we'll have to wait?

(CHORUS)

They say there's someone waiting
for a trim ahead of me.
Can I get you some coffee or some tea?
OK. In the meantime,
I'll be getting something strong
for this headache at the pharmacy!

(CHORUS)

3:37/3:38

A Perfect Dish [Unit 6]

I used to eat a lot of fatty foods,
but now I just avoid them.
I used to like chocolate and lots of sweets,
but now those days are gone.
To tell you the truth,
it was too much trouble.
They say you only live once,
but I'm not crazy about feeling sick.
What was going wrong?
Now I know I couldn't live without this.
Everything's ready.
Why don't you sit down?

(CHORUS)

It looks terrific,
but it smells pretty awful.
What in the world can it be?
It smells like chicken,
and it tastes like fish—
a terrific dish
for you and me—
a perfect dish for you
and me.

I used to be a big meat eater,
now I'm vegetarian,
and I'm not much of a coffee drinker.
I can't stand it anymore.
I'm avoiding desserts with sugar.
I'm trying to lose some weight.
Some things just don't agree with me.
They're bad for me, I'm sure.
Would you like some?
Help yourself.
Isn't it so good for you health?

(CHORUS)

Aren't you going to have some?
Don't you like it?
Wasn't it delicious?
Don't you want some more?

(CHORUS)

4:14/4:15

The Colors of Love [Unit 7]

Are you sick and tired of working hard day and night?
Do you like to look at the world in shades of black and white?
Your life can still be everything that you were dreaming of.
Just take a look around you and see all the colors of love.
You wake up every morning and go through the same old grind.
You don't know how the light at the window could be so unkind. If blue is the color that you choose when the road is rough, you know you really need to believe in the colors of love.

(CHORUS)

The colors of love
are as beautiful as a rainbow.
The colors of love
shine on everyone in the world.

Are negative thoughts and emotions painful to express?
They're just tiny drops in the ocean of happiness.
And these are the feelings you must learn to rise above.
Your whole life is a picture you paint with the colors of love.

(CHORUS)

4:30/4:31

To Each His Own [Unit 8]

He doesn't care for Dali.
The colors are too bright.
He says that Picasso
got everything just right.
She can't stand the movies
that are filmed in Hollywood.
She likes Almodóvar.
She thinks he's really good.
He's inspired by everything
she thinks is second-rate.
She's moved and fascinated
by the things he loves to hate.
He's crazy about art that only
turns her heart to stone.
I guess that's why they say
to each his own.
He likes pencil drawings.
She prefers photographs.
He takes her to the the art museum,
but she just laughs and laughs.
He loves the Da Vinci
that's hanging by the door.
She prefers the modern art
that's lying on the floor.
"No kidding! You'll love it. Just wait and see.
It's perfect in every way."
She shakes her head. "It's not for me.
It's much too old and gray."
She thinks he has the worst taste
that the world has ever known.
I guess that's why they say
to each his own.
But when it's time to say goodbye,
they both feel so alone.
I guess that's why they say
to each his own.

5:17/5:18

Life in Cyberspace [Unit 9]

I'm just fooling around.
Am I interrupting you?
Well, I wanted to know—
what are you up to?
I tried to send some photos,
but it's been so long
that I almost don't remember
how to log on.
So I'm thinking about getting a
new computer.
I don't know what kind. I should have done
it sooner.
But I heard the Panatel is as good as
the rest.
Check it out. Check it out.
You should really check it out.

(CHORUS)

Let's face it—that's life.
That's life in cyberspace.

When you download the pictures,
then you open the files.
If your computer's slow,
then it can take a little while.
From the pull-down menu,
you can print them, too.
But don't forget to save
everything you do.
Scroll it up. Scroll it down.
Put your cursor on the bar.
Then click on the icon,
and you'll see my new car!
The car goes as fast
as the one I had before.
Check it out. Check it out.
You should really check it out.

(CHORUS)

Am I talking to myself, or are you still there?
This instant message conversation's
going nowhere.
I could talk to Liz.
She isn't nearly as nice.
It isn't quite as much fun.
I've done it once or twice.
What's the problem?
Come on. Give it a try.
If you don't want to be friends,
at least tell me why.
Did you leave to make a call
or go out to get some cash?
Did the photos I sent make your
computer crash?

(CHORUS)

5:31/5:32

What Would You Do? [Unit 10]

What would you do
if I got a tattoo with your name?
What would you say
if I dyed my hair for you?
What would you do
if I sang outside your window?
What would you think
if I told you I loved you?

(CHORUS)

I hate to say this,
but I think you're making a big mistake.
By tomorrow,
I'm sure you'll be sorry.

What would you do
if I sent you a love letter?
Would you say it was wrong
and send it back to me?
What would you think
if I pierced my ears? Would you care?
Would you think
that I had lost all my modesty?

(CHORUS)

Well, give it some thought.
I know I could make you happy.
Are you kidding?
You'd have to be nuts to ask me.
It's no mistake. I'm sure
that my heart is yours.
I have to find a way
to make you mine.

(CHORUS)

SECOND EDITION

TOP NOTCH 2A

Workbook

Joan Saslow • Allen Ascher

With Terra Brockman and Julie C. Rouse

PEARSON Longman

UNIT 1

Greetings and Small Talk

Preview

1 **Look at the pictures. Write the correct greeting under each picture. Use words from the box.**

bow	hug	kiss	shake hands

1. ____________

2. ____________

3. ____________

4. ____________

2 **Complete the conversation. Write the letter on the line.**

A: You look familiar. Haven't we met before?
B: ___ (1.)
A: Aren't you from Canada?
B: ___ (2.)
A: I know! I think we met at Joan's house last month.
B: ___ (3.)
A: Yes, that's right. What have you been up to?
B: ___ (4.)
A: Well, it was nice to see you again.
B: ___ (5.)
A: That would be great. Here's my card.

a. Of course! You work with Joan.
b. You, too. We should keep in touch.
c. Not much. Actually, I'm on my way to a class.
d. I don't think so. I'm not from around here.
e. Yes, I am. I'm from Vancouver.

3 **Read the conversation in Exercise 2 again. Circle the subjects the people talk about.**

family   religion   job   age   weather   nationality

4 **When you meet someone new, what subjects do you talk about? Write a ✔ next to the topics you usually talk about. Write an ✗ next to the topics you don't like to talk about.**

___ 1. my family	___ 4. my age	___ 7. politics
___ 2. my religion	___ 5. my hometown or country	___ 8. my job
___ 3. the weather	___ 6. sports	___ 9. other: ____________

5 **Complete each sentence with the present perfect. Use contractions when possible.**

1. A: ______________ (you / have) any coffee today? B: Yes, ______________ (I / have) two cups.
2. A: ______________ (you / be) to Europe? B: Yes, ______________ (we / be) to Spain.
3. A: ______________ (you / exercise) this week? B: Yes, ______________ (I / go) to the gym twice.
4. A: ______________ (you / read) any books lately? B: No, ______________ (I / be) too busy.

6 **Complete the questions with the correct form of the verbs from the box. Use each verb only once. Then write your own responses. When you answer yes, add specific information, using the simple past tense.**

be	check	eat	meet	~~see~~

1. "Have you *seen* ______________ any good movies lately?"
   YOU *Yes, I have. I saw Toy Story 3 last week.*
2. "Have you ______________ any famous people?"
   YOU ______________
3. "Have you ______________ to Europe?"
   YOU ______________
4. "Have you ______________ lunch today?"
   YOU ______________
5. "Have you ______________ your e-mail today?"
   YOU ______________

7 **Complete the conversation with the present perfect or the simple past tense. Use contractions when possible.**

Joe: ______________ (1. you / take) this tour before? I hear it's great.

Trish: Yes, I have. I ______________ (2. come) to Russia with this group two years ago. It ______________ (3. be) a wonderful trip. ______________ (4. you / be) here before?

Joe: Yes, I ______________ (5. visit) Moscow in 2005, but I ______________ (6. not / see) much of the city. It ______________ (7. be) a business trip. I'm really excited about *this* trip!

Trish: Me too. I ______________ (8. read) the brochures several times last night. I can't wait to see all these places again. By the way, ______________ (9. you / meet) Peter, our tour guide?

Joe: No, but I'd like to.

Trish: Come. I'll introduce you.

LESSON 2

8 **Complete the sentences. Circle the correct words.**

1. Have you visited the Louvre (yet / ever)?
2. I haven't been to the opera (already / yet).
3. Who is she? I haven't (ever / before) seen her.
4. Has Evan (yet / ever) tried ceviche (already / before)?
5. We've only been here one day, but we've (already / yet) taken a lot of pictures.
6. My parents have been to Italy (ever / before).
7. Has she (yet / ever) gone sightseeing in New York?
8. Have they (already / before) seen the new Brad Pitt movie?

9 **Complete the conversations. Write questions or answers in the present perfect. Use <u>already</u>, <u>yet</u>, <u>ever</u>, or <u>before</u>.**

1. A: ______________________________?
   B: Yes, he has. George went horseback riding last summer.
2. A: Have Ted and Alice already taken a tour of the Statue of Liberty?
   B: No. They ______________________________.
3. A: ______________________________?
   B: Yes. I've been to London several times.
4. A: ______________________________?
   B: No, but they plan to go to the top of the Sears Tower tomorrow.
5. A: Has Lisa ever tried Turkish coffee?
   B: Yes. She ______________________________.

10 **Look at Anne Marie and Gilbert's to-do list for their vacation in Toronto. Anne Marie has checked what they have already done.**

✓ - take a tour of the university
✓ - meet Michel for dinner on Spadina Avenue
- visit the Bata Shoe Museum
✓ - see a musical downtown
- take a boat trip around Toronto Harbor
✓ - go shopping at the Eaton Centre

Now finish Anne Marie's postcard to her friend. Write what she and Gilbert have already done and what they haven't done yet. Use the present perfect.

Dear Agnes, Sunday, August 6

Gilbert and I are having a wonderful time in Toronto.
We've done so many things! ______________________
____
____
____
____
____
____
____
____

See you when we get back.

Love,
Anne Marie

LESSON 3

11 Extra reading comprehension

Read the article on page 8 in the Student's Book again. Answer the questions.

1. What is "body talk"? ______________________
2. How should you greet someone in France? ______________________
3. Where is hugging common during introductions? ______________________
4. What does the "OK" sign mean in Japan? ______________________
5. What advice does the article give? ______________________

12 **Read the information about greetings in Asia. Then read the statements and check true, false, or no information.**

GETTING GREETINGS RIGHT

The traditional greeting in Asia is a bow. In fact, there are different types of bows used in greetings throughout Asia. For example, in Japan, China, and Korea, people bow, but in Japan the bow is usually lower. In India and nearby countries in South Asia, most people put their hands together and bow just a little.

While each Asian culture has its own traditional special greeting, these days, don't be surprised if people in Asia just shake your hand.

	true	false	no information
1. People in China, Japan, and Korea bow when they greet someone.	☐	☐	☐
2. In Korea, people usually bow lower than in Japan.	☐	☐	☐
3. In India, you shouldn't touch the person you are greeting.	☐	☐	☐
4. People in many places in South Asia use a similar greeting.	☐	☐	☐

13 **Complete the sentences about yourself.**

1. In this country, the most common greeting is ____________________.
2. When I greet someone for the first time, I usually ____________________.
3. When I greet a family member or close friend, I usually ____________________.

FACTOID

History of the Handshake

Shaking hands was a way of making sure that people were not carrying a weapon such as a knife or sword. When you shook hands, you were saying, "Look, I don't have a weapon. I trust you. Let's be friends."

LESSON 4

14 **Complete the chart. Write things you've done and things you haven't done but would like to do.**

	Things I've done	Things I'd like to do
climb	climb Mt. Kilimanjaro	climb Mt. Everest

	Things I've done	Things I'd like to do
climb		
visit		
go sightseeing in		
learn		
go to the top of		
see		
try		
meet		
take a tour of		

15 **CHALLENGE. Look at your experiences in Exercise 14. Write about three things you've done using <u>already</u> or <u>before</u>. Describe each experience with a participial adjective.**

I've already climbed Mt. Kilimanjaro in Tanzania. It was thrilling!

1. ______________________________
2. ______________________________
3. ______________________________

Now write about three things you haven't done but would like to do. Use <u>yet</u>, <u>have never</u>, or <u>haven't ever</u>.

1. ______________________________
2. ______________________________
3. ______________________________

GRAMMAR BOOSTER

A **Look at the answers. Write information questions, using the question words in parentheses.**

1. A: (Where) ______________________________?
   B: He's lived in Santiago, Budapest, and Kyoto.
2. A: (How) ______________________________?
   B: It's been great—sunny and warm every day!
3. A: (What) ______________________________?
   B: Sophie has studied English, Spanish, and Japanese.
4. A: (Which) ______________________________?
   B: They've gone to the Metropolitan Museum of Art and the Museum of Modern Art.
5. A: (How many) ______________________________?
   B: She's been to Paris three times.
6. A: (Who) ______________________________?
   B: I've met Mr. Russ, Mr. Sherman, and Ms. Savidge.

B **Rewrite each sentence, changing the placement of <u>yet</u> or <u>already</u>.**

1. We've taken that tour already. ______________________________
2. They haven't yet climbed Mt. McKinley. ______________________________
3. Has he eaten dinner already? ______________________________
4. I've already gone sightseeing in Prague. ______________________________
5. She hasn't tried Vietnamese food yet. ______________________________

C **Complete the sentences. Circle the correct words.**

1. Have you (yet / already) taken pictures of the City of Arts and Sciences building?
2. Josefina hasn't had her lunch (yet / already).
3. Ryan has finished college (yet / already).
4. Has Michelle (ever / before) been to Greece?
5. My parents have (ever / never) gone on a cruise.
6. I haven't (ever / never) studied Italian.
7. Ruth has (ever / never) tried duck before.
8. Simone is from Paris, but she's never (ever / before) gone to the top of the Eiffel Tower!

City of Arts and Sciences—Valencia, Spain

D **Think of a frightening, a thrilling, a fascinating, and a disgusting experience. Write questions with ever.**

1. frightening: *Have you ever jumped out of an airplane?*

1. frightening: ______
2. thrilling: ______
3. fascinating: ______
4. disgusting: ______

Now write short answers to your questions.

1. ______
2. ______
3. ______
4. ______

E **CHALLENGE. What are four things that you've never done? Write sentences using the words in parentheses.**

1. (never) ______
2. (not ever) ______
3. (never, before) ______
4. (never, ever) ______

WRITING BOOSTER

A **Read the run-on sentences. Write each sentence correctly. Separate the independent clauses with a period or combine them with a coordinating conjunction, such as and or but.**

1. My parents went on a cruise to the Bahamas they haven't been to Bermuda yet.

____

____

2. I've been to the top of the CN Tower, the view is amazing.

____

____

3. They went skiing in the Himalayas, the trip was thrilling.

____

____

4. I've tried snails before they were disgusting.

____

____

5. Devin has never traveled to continental Europe he has visited Ireland before.

____

____

6. We have met before we were on the same sightseeing tour yesterday.

____

____

7. He's from Russia, he has studied English, he would like to learn Mandarin.

____

____

B **Look at Exercise C on page 11 in the Student's Book. On a separate sheet of paper, write your partner's experience. Describe what happened, where your partner was, who your partner was with, and how he or she felt.**

C **After you write about your partner's experience in Exercise B, check to see if you have written any run-on sentences. Be sure to use a period to separate the independent clauses or use connecting words to combine them.**

UNIT 2

Movies and Entertainment

Preview

1 Complete the sentences with words or expressions from the box.

a bunch of	Frankly	I can't stand	It's my treat	I've heard

1. There are ______________ good new comedies on Netclips. I can't decide which one to watch.
2. ______________ the new Leonardo DiCaprio movie is fantastic. Have you seen it yet?
3. I have two tickets for the 10:00 show. Would you like to go? ______________.
4. *Titanic?* ______________, I'm too tired for a three-hour romantic epic!
5. ______________ horror movies. I watch movies to relax—not to be frightened.

2 Answer the questions about your own movie preferences.

1. What actor or actress are you a big fan of? ______________
2. What movie genres are you usually in the mood for? ______________
3. What was the last movie you saw in a theater? ______________
4. What was the last movie you watched at home? ______________

LESSON 1

3 Complete the posting from an online movie message board. Use <u>since</u> or <u>for</u>.

Movie Reviews

Back | Forward | Reload | Stop | Home | Search

ONLINE MOVIE REVIEWS

Actors
Links
Schedule
Discussion Board

Name: Veeck
Date: 7/10 8:12 A.M.
Post # 5

Comments: I've been an action film fan ________ (1.) 20 years, ________ (2.) I was 10 years old. I haven't seen a good one ________ (3.) a very long time. Last night I saw the movie *Robin Hood* and it was terrible. I watched it for about an hour but then I had to turn it off. I kept falling asleep!! It was the worst action film I've seen ________ (4.) 1991, when I saw *Rambo*. In my opinion, there still haven't been any good action films ________ (5.) *Avatar* in 2009. What a disappointment!

4 **Look at the pictures. Then complete the conversation.**

Patty: Hi, Rosemary. Sorry I'm late. Have you been here long?

Rosemary: For about twenty minutes. What happened?

Patty: First ____________________ (1.). I ran to catch it, but it pulled away. And ____________________ (2.), because it was raining. So, I went back home to get my car. Then ____________________ (3.). Finally I got here, but ____________________ (4.). It took me about ten minutes before I found one!

Rosemary: Well, you're here now. Let's go see the movie!

LESSON 2

5 **Match each movie genre with the correct description. Write the letter on the line.**

1. ____ feature fast-paced, exciting, and dangerous situations	a.	dramas
2. ____ are drawn by hand or created on a computer	b.	documentaries
3. ____ tell a story with singing and dancing	c.	science-fiction films
4. ____ give us information about real people and things	d.	action films
5. ____ usually take place in the future	e.	animated films
6. ____ make us smile and laugh	f.	musicals
7. ____ focus on characters' problems and emotions	g.	comedies

6 **Read the newspaper movie listings. Write the genre that best describes each movie.**

ESSEX TIMES

Friday, May 22 — ENTERTAINMENT — page 39

The Fearless Fighter

You'll be on the edge of your seat. Don't miss this exciting adventure! But don't bring the kids—a little too violent.

Edgewood Theater: 6:00, 8:15, 10:30

Myra's Day

Spend the day with Myra. You'll laugh so hard you might fall out of your seat!

Plaza Cinemas: 4:00, 6:00, 8:00

Goodnight, Mariana

Mariana tries to find her long lost mother. Her search takes her all over the country. Very sad and touching. Based on a true story.

Castle Theater: 4:00, 6:15, 8:30

Genre: ____________ Genre: ____________ Genre: ____________

7 **CHALLENGE. Which of the movies from the listing in Exercise 6 would you rather see? Explain your answer.**

8 **Look at Tom's favorite things and <u>least</u> favorite things. Then read each statement and check <u>true</u> or <u>false</u>, based on Tom's lists.**

Tom's Favorite Things

1. comedies
2. a trip to the beach
3. pop music
4. going to the gym
5. rice

Tom's <u>Least</u> Favorite Things

1. documentaries
2. a trip to the mountains
3. classical music
4. going shopping
5. pasta

	true	false
1. Tom would rather see a comedy than a documentary.	☐	☐
2. He'd rather take a trip to the mountains than to the beach.	☐	☐
3. He'd rather listen to classical music than pop music.	☐	☐
4. He'd rather go to the gym than go shopping.	☐	☐
5. Tom would rather eat rice than pasta.	☐	☐

9 **Look at the statements in Exercise 8. Write five true statements about your own preferences. Use <u>would rather</u>.**

10 **Read the online movie reviews. Then complete the chart. Write the genre and choose two adjectives from the box to describe each movie. Circle "thumbs up" if the reviewer recommends the movie or "thumbs down" if he or she doesn't recommend it.**

boring	hilarious	interesting	silly	unforgettable	violent	weird

The Movies

File Edit Links Tools Help Chat

THE REVIEW PAGES

THE ALIEN!

I was really looking forward to this: Martians take over a city in the year 2020. I usually love these kinds of movies, but *The Alien!* is just too strange for words. The story doesn't make sense. It was downright stupid!

—Kris Baker

SEARCH FOR THE LOST KINGDOM

This is going to be a blockbuster hit! The acting was terrific! A little too much killing for me, but it was still a great movie. I won't forget this movie for a long time!

—Ajay007

DAD'S BACK!

In *Dad's Back!*, Moran Silva films himself and his real family for a whole month. It sounds boring, but you'll be surprised at how entertaining the movie is. I strongly recommend this film to anyone looking for a good laugh.

—Marty19

DON'T SCREAM NOW

A film about a killer monster is scary and exciting, right? Not this one! It was not interesting at all! Almost everyone gets killed, and still I couldn't stay awake! I'd rather have stayed home and read a book.

—Yasir

ONLINE

Movie title	Genre	Adjectives	Reviewer's opinion
The Alien!			
Search for the Lost Kingdom			
Dad's Back!			
Don't Scream Now			

11 **Complete the conversation. Write the letter on the line.**

A: Hi, Janelle. Seen any good movies recently?

B: ___ 1.

A: *Play Time*? What kind of movie is that?

B: ___ 2.

A: Well, what is it about?

B: ___ 3.

A: That doesn't sound very funny. Was it any good?

B: ___ 4.

A: The funniest? Wow! Who was in it?

B: ___ 5.

A: So you think I would like it?

B: ___ 6.

a. It was terrific. It might be the funniest film I've seen this year.

b. It's a comedy.

c. Definitely. I highly recommend it.

d. Yeah, I just saw *Play Time* at the Art Cinema.

e. It's about some high school kids who don't want to graduate.

f. It stars Wilson Grant—he was really hilarious.

12 **CHALLENGE. Write your own review about a movie you've seen. Use the reviews in Exercise 10 for support. In your review, answer the following questions: What kind of movie was it? Who was in it? What was it about? Was it funny? Romantic? Thought-provoking? Would you recommend it?**

LESSON 4

13 Extra reading comprehension

Read the article *Can Violent Movies or TV Programs Harm Children?* on page 22 in the Student's Book again. Then read each statement and check <u>true</u> or <u>false</u>, according to the information in the article.

		true	false
1.	It's OK for children to watch violence in animated TV shows and movies.	☐	☐
2.	Children who watch a lot of fighting and killing on TV are more likely to act violently as adults.	☐	☐
3.	Eight is a safe age for children to start watching violent movies and TV shows.	☐	☐
4.	Violence is normal, so children should be exposed to it.	☐	☐
5.	Children should learn that there are consequences for doing bad things.	☐	☐
6.	Parents should watch and discuss violent TV programs with their very young children.	☐	☐

14 **Read the online blog post. Then answer the questions.**

How can I protect my kids from media violence?

08 APR 2011 10:05 PM

POST A COMMENT

James F

view profile

The forecast is for rain all weekend, so I thought I'd get some movies for the kids to watch. When we got to the video store, my nine-year-old son headed straight for the new releases. Every video he picked had a gun or an explosion on the cover. My six-year-old brought me a movie based on one of his favorite toys. He begged me to rent it, "Please, Dad. I have the toys. Why can't I see the movie?" But this movie is not for children. According to the reviews I've read, it's very scary and pretty bloody. We came home with a popular animated film I found in the family section, but even that had fighting in it. And the violent scenes were also silly and funny. Frankly, I think that's sending kids a bad message.

I was so upset that I decided to do some research on children and media violence. Did you know that between the ages of four and eighteen, the average child sees 200,000 acts of violence on TV and other media—including 40,000 murders? Also, 60 to 90% of the most popular video games have violent subject matter. Another study found that 61% of television programs show some violence, and 43% of these violent scenes are used to make people laugh!

Why can't the entertainment industry make kids' movies and TV shows that are actually appropriate for kids? And when will they stop selling toys based on violent movies and video games that young children should not see or play? Maybe next time it rains, I'll take my kids to the library instead!

Source: mediafamily.org

1. What is James F.'s nine-year-old son interested in? ______
2. What does his six-year-old want to see? ______
3. What does James F. rent? ______
4. Why is he upset? ______
5. What does he think the entertainment industry should do? ______
______
6. Do you agree with James F.? Explain your answer. ______
______

15 **Complete the statements, according to the blog post in Exercise 14. Circle the letter.**

1. Between the ages of four and eighteen, the average child sees _____ on TV and in other media.
   a. 40,000 television programs b. 200,000 murders c. 40,000 murders
2. _____ of all TV shows contain violent scenes.
   a. More than half b. Half c. Less than half
3. Violence on TV is often meant to be seen as _____.
   a. unforgettable b. funny c. scary

GRAMMAR BOOSTER

A **Read the sentence in column A. Then decide if the sentence in column B is true or false.**

	A	B	true	false
1.	She's been living in Milan for two years.	She still lives in Milan.	☐	☐
2.	He's lived in Quito since 2009.	He doesn't live in Quito now.	☐	☐
3.	I've climbed Mt. Sorak.	I am climbing Mt. Sorak now.	☐	☐
4.	How long have you been reading that book?	You are still reading the book.	☐	☐
5.	She's written a review of the new movie.	She's finished writing the review.	☐	☐
6.	We've been waiting to see *Avatar.*	We've already seen *Avatar.*	☐	☐

B **Think of three activities that you enjoy. When did you start? For each activity, write one present perfect sentence and one present perfect continuous sentence. Use for or since.**

I've played the piano for three years. I've been playing the piano for three years.

C **Complete each statement with the present perfect continuous.**

1. I ______________ (hear) really good things about the new Keira Knightley movie.
2. Jimmy ______________ (give) me DVDs to watch on the weekends.
3. *Ski Trip* ______________ (get) terrible reviews.
4. *Planet X* ______________ (make) a lot of money since it came out last week.
5. Audrey's grandparents ______________ (pay) for her acting classes.
6. Joe and Clem ______________ (travel) around Europe and Asia for nine months.
7. We ______________ (look) for a movie for a half hour. Just choose something!

D **Complete the sentences. Circle the correct words.**

1. I (prefer / would rather) see a silly movie than a violent movie.
2. Annabelle (likes / would rather) classic films.
3. We (prefer / would rather) to order tickets online.
4. She would (like / rather) to watch a romantic comedy.
5. Would you (prefer / rather) sit in the middle or on the aisle?
6. No soda for me. I (prefer / would rather) water.
7. Oscar (prefers / would rather) not go to the movies tonight.

E **Look at the answers. Write questions with <u>like</u>, <u>prefer</u>, or <u>would</u> <u>rather</u>. There is more than one correct answer.**

1. **A:** ______________________________?
   B: A drama. I'm not that big on musicals.
2. **A:** ______________________________?
   B: Popcorn, please. I don't eat candy.
3. **A:** ______________________________?
   B: Definitely a movie. Plays are fine, but I really love movies.
4. **A:** ______________________________?
   B: Saturday works for me. I'm busy on Sunday.
5. **A:** ______________________________?
   B: I'm not in the mood for Chinese food. What about Mexican?
6. **A:** ______________________________?
   B: It doesn't matter to me. You choose.

WRITING BOOSTER

A **Write a topic sentence for the following paragraph.**

Topic sentence: ______________________________

People don't imitate the behavior they see in movies. Would you try jumping from the roof of one tall building to another because you saw it in an action film? We live in a violent world. Just open any newspaper—or history book. What happens in real life is more violent than what happens in movies, and violence is not new. Violent entertainment has been around for a long time. Think about the gladiators in ancient Rome.

B **Why do some people think violence in movies is harmful? Why do others think it isn't? Complete the chart with people's opinions. Look at Exercise A above and the article on page 22 of the Student's Book for ideas.**

Violence in movies	
Harmful	**Not harmful**
Can make children more aggressive	

C **On a separate sheet of paper, write two paragraphs of three to five sentences each with details about the following topics. Then write and add a topic sentence for each paragraph.**

Paragraph 1
The best movie you ever saw and why you liked it.

Paragraph 2
The worst movie you ever saw and why you couldn't stand it.

UNIT 3

Staying in Hotels

Preview

1 **Look at the hotel bill. Then answer the questions.**

Mr. Philip Paul
11 Rue Ravignan
Place Emil Goudeau
75018 Paris, France
CLUB ONE MEMBER # PP2139

ROOM 1631
ARRIVAL 09/14
DEPARTURE 09/16
TIME 15:52

NOVA HOTEL

DATE	REFERENCE	DESCRIPTION	AMOUNT
9/14	13:13	Local Call	Free (Club One member)
9/14	08:32	Overseas Call	40.34
9/14	3036	Internet access	Free (Club One member)
9/14	2765	Laundry	36.00
9/14		Room 1631	179.00
9/14	3036	Internet access	Free (Club One member)
9/14	2762	Room Service	18.92
9/15	2762	Room Service	26.45
9/15	09:52	Local Call	Free (Club One member)
9/15	428	Photocopies	Free (Club One member)
9/15	3036	Internet access	Free (Club One member)
9/15	758	Local Fax	Free (Club One member)
9/15		Room 1631	179.00
9/15	09562	Airport Shuttle	30.00
		BALANCE	509.71
		VAT 7.00%	35.68
		TOTAL INCLUDING VAT	545.39

1. What date did Mr. Paul check in? ____________________
2. How much did he pay for phone calls, faxes, and Internet service? ____________________
3. How many nights did Mr. Paul stay at the hotel? ____________________
4. What is the total amount of the hotel bill? ____________________

2 **Check the hotel services that Mr. Paul used at the Nova Hotel, according to the hotel bill.**

☐ 

☐ 

☐ 

☐ 

☐ 

☐ 

☐ 

☐ 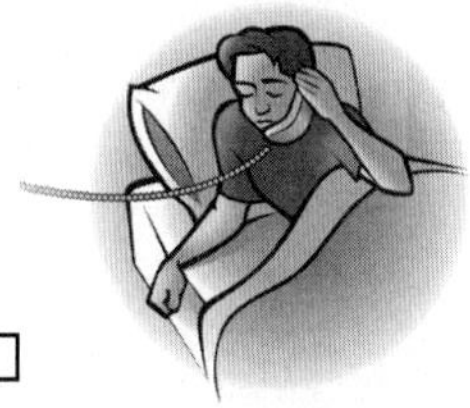

☐ 

☐ 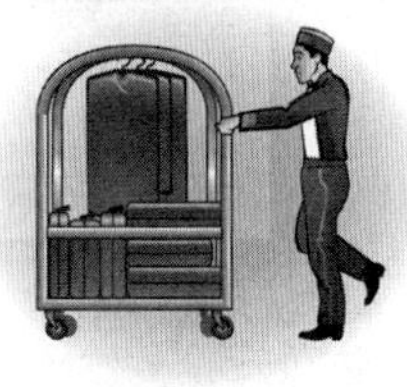

3 **Which services are important to these hotel guests? Read what each person says and write the hotel service on the line.**

I like to have breakfast in my room before I get dressed for the day.

1. ____________________

I need child care so that my wife and I can go out at night.

2. ____________________

I have a very important meeting in the morning. I can't oversleep!

3. ____________________

I check e-mail and work on my laptop in the evening.

4. ____________________

I would rather swim for exercise than lift weights.

5. ____________________

I want someone to make restaurant and sightseeing reservations for me.

6. ____________________

LESSON 1

4 **Look at the pictures and complete the sentences with <u>'d better</u> or <u>'d better not</u>.**

1. "Hey, look at that sign. We ____________________ ____________________________________."

2. "Blackbird is a very popular restaurant. You ____________________________________."

3. "It's after midnight. We ______________
____
______________________."

4. "The movie starts in three minutes.
You ______________________
______________________."

5 Complete the conversations. Write responses with had better.

1. A: It's 10:45. Check out is at 11:00.
   B: ______________________
2. A: The items in the minibar are really expensive.
   B: ______________________
3. A: Oh, no! I left my purse at the restaurant.
   B: ______________________
4. A: It's a popular movie. Tickets might sell out.
   B: ______________________
5. A: This is a double room. We're a family of five!
   B: ______________________
6. A: The hotel offers a free breakfast, but it's only until 9:00.
   B: ______________________
7. A: The sauna is for adults only.
   B: ______________________

LESSON 2

6 Put the conversation in order. Write the number on the line.

__1__ Can I speak with Kevin Mercer, please? He's staying in room 376.

_____ That's right.

_____ Yes. Could you tell him Barbara called? Please ask him to call me back at 555–3156.

_____ One moment, please . . . I'm sorry. There's no answer. Can I take a message?

_____ Barbara at 555–3156?

_____ Is that all?

__7__ Yes, that's it. Thank you very much.

7 The fortune-teller is predicting the future. Read her predictions. Then rewrite the sentences using will.

1. ______________________________
2. ______________________________
3. ______________________________
4. ______________________________
5. ______________________________

8 Rewrite the following future statements and questions using will.

1. I'm going to call her later today. ______________________________
2. She's going to stop at the front desk first. ______________________________
3. My uncle is meeting my father at the airport. ______________________________
4. What time does the tour group get back? ______________________________
5. When are they going to make a reservation? ______________________________
6. Where is your grandmother staying in Madrid? ______________________________

9 Read the phone conversation. Then complete the message sheet.

A: Hello. I'd like to speak with Ms. Marina Santiago, please.

B: One moment, please. I'll ring Ms. Santiago's room . . . I'm sorry, but there's no answer. Would you like to call back later?

A: No, I'd like to leave a message. Please tell her that Anna Streed called. I'll be at 555–8723 until 5:00 today.

B: OK, Ms. Anna Street . . .

A: No, it's Streed, S-T-R-E-E-D—that's "D" as in "door."

B: OK, Ms. Streed. I'll make sure she gets the message.

To Marina Santiago

Date 9/14 Time 3:15 A.M. ☐ P.M. ☒

WHILE YOU WERE OUT

☐ Mr./ ☐ Ms./ ☐ Mrs. ______________

Phone ______________
Area code Number Extension

☐ telephoned ☐ please call
☐ returned your call ☐ will call back

Message: ______________

10 Label the pictures.

11 Look at the pictures. Then complete the conversations.

1. A: Guest services. May I help you?

B: Yes, please. Could you bring up some ______________ ?
(1.)

A: Certainly.

B: And I could use a ______________ , too. My hair is wet, and I don't see one in the bathroom.
(2.)

A: Sure. We'll bring those up right away. Anything else?

B: Oh, yes. I have a lot of dirty clothes. Could someone please ______________ ?
(3.)

A: Yes, of course.

B: I think that's all. Thanks!

2. A: Front Desk. May I help you?

B: Yes, I'd like to go for a swim. Is the ______________ still open?
(4.)

A: No, I'm sorry, it closed at 9:00.

B: Oh. Well, maybe a workout. How about the ______________ ?
(5.)

A: No, it also just closed.

B: Oh, no. Well, I guess I'll have to do some work then. Is the ______________ still open?
(6.)

A: No, I'm sorry, it closed at 6:30. But you do have high-speed Internet access in your room.

B: Oh, OK. Thanks.

LESSON 4

12 Extra reading comprehension

Read *Where to Stay in New York* on page 34 of the Student's Book again. Then read the statements and check true, false, or no information.

	true	false	no information
1. The Plaza is the most expensive hotel.	☐	☐	☐
2. The Casablanca Hotel is in the Theater District.	☐	☐	☐
3. The Hotel Chelsea has suites.	☐	☐	☐
4. The Peninsula is a budget hotel.	☐	☐	☐
5. The Broadway Inn is noisy.	☐	☐	☐
6. The Habitat Hotel is pet friendly.	☐	☐	☐

13 **Read the travel guide about places to stay in Dublin, Ireland.**

SLEEPING IN DUBLIN

Very expensive / Moderately priced / Budget

The Shelbourne Hotel

History, Location

Built in 1824, the Shelbourne is the most famous hotel in Dublin and a home-away-from-home for generations of politicians, writers, and actors. In fact, in 1922 the Irish Constitution was written in Room 112! Overlooking Saint Stephen's Green public park in the heart of Dublin, the location is perfect for sightseeing and shopping. Even if you don't stay here, you must go for afternoon tea in the elegant Lord Mayor's Lounge.

restaurant, room service, laundry service, business center, Internet service

The Morgan Hotel

Style, Nightlife

If you're crazy about style, the Morgan Hotel is your place. With very modern décor and designer furniture, this chic hotel is a favorite of people who work in fashion and music. The Morgan is located in the trendy Temple Bar district—an area popular with young people and *the* center of nightlife in Dublin. Note: Can be noisy at night.

restaurant, room service, laundry service, business center, Internet service, fitness room

The Aberdeen Lodge

Atmosphere, Service

A short train ride from the Dublin city center, in a neighborhood of beautiful old homes and gardens, the Aberdeen Lodge is the perfect place for a quiet and relaxing stay. The friendly staff welcomes guests with tea and cookies and is very helpful with tourist advice. Suites feature working fireplaces. Don't miss breakfast in the lovely dining room overlooking the garden. Note: There is no elevator.

restaurant, room service, laundry service

The Camden Court

Convenience, Location

The Camden Court is a large hotel that offers business travelers a good night's sleep and lot of amenities at an affordable price. Rooms are small but clean and comfortable. A short walk from Saint Stephen's Green, the location is perfect—close to tourist attractions, restaurants, and shopping. The Camden Court is a good choice for business or pleasure.

pool, sauna, fitness room, room service, business center, free Internet service, beauty salon, restaurant, free parking

Trinity College

Price, Location

Experience student life—without the exams!—at this beautiful, historic university located in the center of Dublin. From June to September, visitors can reserve single and double rooms while students are away for the summer holiday. Rooms are large and clean, but don't expect many amenities or services. Not all rooms have their own bathrooms.

cafeteria-style restaurant, free breakfast

Source: *Lonely Planet Dublin City Guide*

14 **Complete the chart. Use the travel guide in Exercise 13 to list an advantage and a disadvantage of each hotel.**

Hotel	Advantage	Disadvantage
The Shelbourne Hotel		
The Morgan Hotel		
The Aberdeen Lodge		
The Camden Court		
Trinity College		

15 **Read about the people's hotel needs and preferences. Use the travel guide in Exercise 13 to decide where the people should or shouldn't stay. Write statements with had better (not) or should (not).**

I want to meet other people my age and walk to clubs at night.

1. ______________________________

Peter broke his leg, but we can't change our flight. We need to be close to the sights and comfortable.

2. ______________________________

I'm traveling in the summer. Location is important to me, but I'm on a budget.

3. ______________________________

I'm attending a conference in Dublin. I'll have to wake up early, so I'd like someplace quiet. Oh, and I've got to be able to exercise.

4. ______________________________

GRAMMAR BOOSTER

A **Write sentences. Use have to, must not, don't have to, or doesn't have to.**

1. Employees and guests / smoke in the hotel ______
2. Hotel guests / check out before noon ______
3. A guest / use anything from the minibar ______
4. Hotel maids / make up the rooms ______
5. Hotel guests / reuse their towels, but they can ______
6. We / forget to unplug the iron ______

B **Read the situation. Write a suggestion. Use could, should, ought to, shouldn't, had better, or had better not.**

1. The 7:00 show is sold out. ______
2. We have a lot of luggage. ______
3. It's expensive to take a taxi to the airport. ______
4. The play starts at 8:00. ______
5. The Peninsula Hotel is very expensive. ______
6. We don't know where to go for dinner. ______

C **Write a rule for each place. Use be supposed to or not supposed to.**

1. a hospital: *You're not supposed to use your cell phone in a hospital.*
2. a restaurant: ______
3. a movie theater: ______
4. an airplane: ______
5. a museum: ______
6. the library: ______

D **Complete the conversation using will or won't. Use contractions when possible.**

A: ______ (1.) you be staying with us another night?

B: No, we ______ (2.). But I think we ______ (3.) be back next month.

A: Great. How ______ (4.) you be paying today?

B: I ______ (5.) use my credit card, if that's OK.

A: Sure. That ______ (6.) be fine.

E Look at the pictures. What do you think the man is going to do? Write sentences with a form of <u>be going to</u> or <u>not be going to</u>.

1. ______________________________ ______________________________

2. ______________________________ ______________________________

3. ______________________________ ______________________________

4. ______________________________ ______________________________

5. ______________________________ ______________________________

F Complete the conversations. Use the correct form of <u>be going to</u> if there is a plan for the future or <u>will</u> if there is not a plan.

1. **A:** Have you decided about your vacation yet?

   B: Yes, we have. We ____________ (1. go) to India!

   A: Wow! When ____________ you ____________ (2. leave)?

   B: We ____________ (3. fly) out on the 20th.

   A: That's fantastic. Where ____________ you ____________ (4. stay)?

   B: I don't know yet. I guess we should make hotel reservations—or maybe we ____________ just ____________ (5. find) something when we arrive.

2. **A:** Guess what? I ____________ (6. move) into a new apartment next week.

   B: That's great news! I ____________ (7. help) you if you like. What day ____________ you ____________ (8. move)?

   A: Thanks! It's this Saturday at 9 A.M. OK?

   B: Oh, no! I ____________ (9. pick up) my sister at the airport then.

   A: No problem. Just come by when you're free.

A **Read the hotel reviews in Exercise 13 on page 22 again. Complete each statement with a reason, according to the information in the reviews. Write the letter on the line.**

1. _____ I prefer the Shelbourne . . .
2. _____ I'm going to stay at the Morgan . . .
3. _____ I'd like to stay at the Aberdeen Lodge . . .
4. _____ I'd rather stay at the Camden Court . . .
5. _____ I chose Trinity College . . .

a. because I'm not that big on noisy cities.
b. since I'm looking for the cheapest accommodations.
c. because I'm interested in Irish history.
d. since I want to be in Temple Bar.
e. since I'm going to rent a car.

B **Rewrite the sentences in Exercise A, placing the dependent clause at the beginning of each sentence. Use a comma.**

1. ______________________________
2. ______________________________
3. ______________________________
4. ______________________________
5. ______________________________

C **Look at the hotel reviews in Exercise 13. Which hotel would you rather stay at? Write the name of the hotel in the circle. List reasons with because or since in the boxes.**

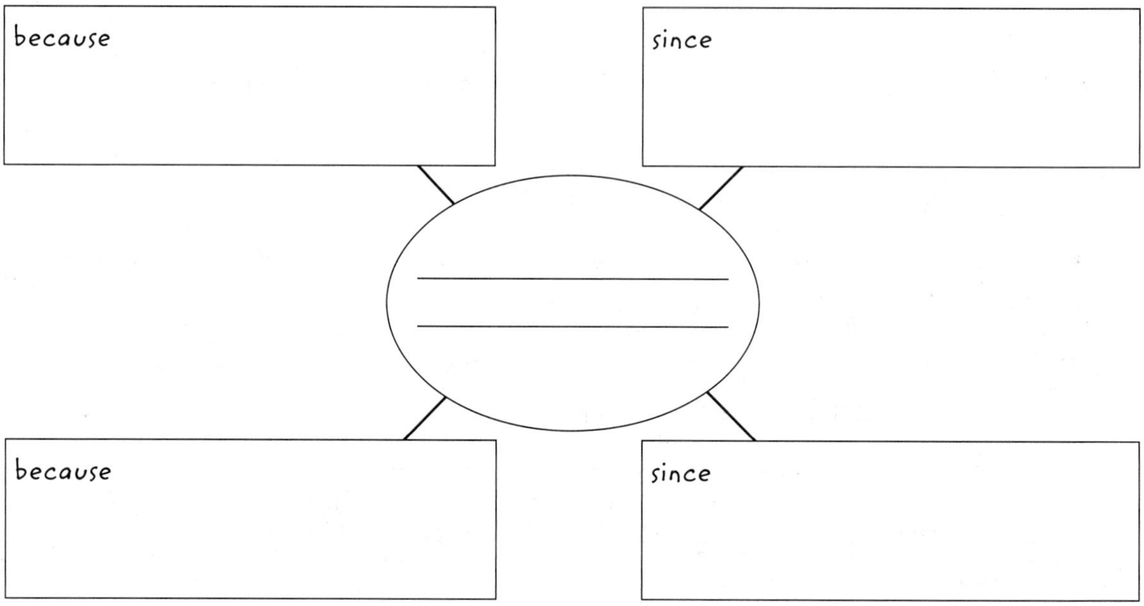

D **On a separate sheet of paper, write a paragraph about the hotel you chose in Exercise C. Explain why you would like to stay there. Give reasons, using because or since. Are there any disadvantages? After you write your paragraph, check carefully to make sure that there are no sentence fragments.**

UNIT 4

Cars and Driving

Preview

1 **Complete each sentence with a car type from the box.**

a convertible	a minivan	an SUV	a luxury car	a compact car

1. Mavis loves hiking. She has ________________ with four-wheel drive that she can drive on rough roads when she takes a trip to the mountains.
2. If you just need a car that's small and easy to park, ________________ would be great for you.
3. Mrs. Jeter drives ________________ to take her husband to work and their five children to school every morning.
4. Peter thinks that owning ________________ is really cool. He said, "You can have the roof down and enjoy the sun, wind, and beautiful sky when the weather is nice."
5. Jack is the president of a big company and he drives ________________ with expensive leather seats.

2 **Read the phone conversation. Then complete the rental form.**

Agent: Good afternoon. L & M Car Rental. How can I help you?

Renter: Hello. I'd like to make a reservation for June 10th.

Agent: Certainly. What type of car do you need?

Renter: A compact car.

Agent: Let's see . . . I'm afraid I don't have a compact available for that date. Is a full-size sedan OK?

Renter: That's fine.

Agent: How long do you need the car for?

Renter: For eight days. Can I pick up the car here in Middletown and return it at Bradley Airport?

Agent: Yes, that's fine. But there is a drop-off fee for one-way rentals.

Renter: All right. One last question: where are you located?

Agent: We're at 355 South Street in Middletown.

L & M Car Rental Agency, Ltd.

Pick up date: ________________

Pick up location: ________________

Drop off date: ________________

Drop off location: ________________

3 **Choose the correct response. Circle the letter.**

1. "How may I help you?"
   a. I have a reservation. b. Just a moment. c. That's right.
2. "The name is Suman Patel."
   a. We were expecting you. b. You're all set. c. That's all ready to go.
3. "Do you need a wagon or a minivan?"
   a. That's correct. b. Certainly, sir. c. Either way.
4. "Could I see your driver's license?"
   a. Here you go. b. No, I don't. c. Here are the keys.
5. "I have you picking up the car on April 12th."
   a. I don't have it with me. b. That's correct. c. Either way.

LESSON 1

4 **Label the car parts.**

1. d a s h b o a r d
2. _ _ _ _ _ _ _ _ _ _ _ _ _ _
3. _ _ _ _ _ _ _ _ _ _ _ _ _ _
4. _ _ _ _
5. _ _ _ _ _ _ _ _ _
6. _ _ _ _ _ _ _ _ _ _ _ _ _ _
7. _ _ _ _ _ _ _ _
8. _ _ _ _ _ _ _ _ _
9. _ _ _ _ _ _ _ _ _ _ _
10. _ _ _ _ _ _

5 **Complete the conversation with the past continuous or the simple past tense.**

A: Hi, Sandra. What's wrong?

B: I _______________ (1. have) an accident on the way home today.

A: Oh, no! How _______________ it _______________ (2. happen)?

B: Well, I _______________ (3. drive) home when my sister _______________ (4. call). She _______________ (5. ask) what I _______________ (6. do), and I _______________ (7. tell) her I _______________ (8. go) home and would see her soon. But she _______________ (9. say) she had a funny story that she just <u>had</u> to tell me. Anyway, by the end of the story, I _______________ (10. laugh) so hard I couldn't see—and I _______________ (11. drive) right into a stop sign.

6 **Choose the correct response. Write the letter on the line.**

1. "I had an accident today." _____
2. "Are you OK?" _____
3. "How did it happen?" _____
4. "Luckily, I was wearing my seat belt." _____
5. "Was there much damage?" _____

a. The other driver was speeding.
b. Not really. The other driver will have to replace a taillight.
c. Thank goodness.
d. Yes, I'm fine. No one was hurt.
e. How awful.

7 **CHALLENGE. Have you or has someone you know ever had an accident? What happened? Write a note to a friend about it.**

LESSON 2

8 **Look at the pictures. Write the letter of the correct picture after each phrasal verb.**

1. fill up ____ 2. turn on ____ 3. drop off ____ 4. turn off ____ 5. pick up ____

9 **CHALLENGE. Complete the note below. Use the correct phrasal verb from Exercise 8. Sometimes you will need to use direct object pronouns.**

Hi, Lisa!

I made an appointment to have Stan fix the car today. Can you ____________ (1.) at the service station this afternoon? Tell Stan that the left turn signal isn't working. This morning I could ____________ (2.), but now it's stuck, and I can't seem to ____________ (3.). Ask him to call me when the car is done. I'll ____________ (4.) on my way home from work.

Love, Daniel

P.S. While you're there, could you ____________ (5.) the tank? See you tonight!

10 **Choose the correct response. Circle the letter.**

1. "I'm dropping off my rental car."
   a. It's all ready to go. b. Was everything OK? c. Was there much damage?
2. "Any problems?"
   a. I just filled it up. b. The sunroof won't open. c. I'm sorry to hear that.
3. "What's wrong with the air conditioning?"
   a. It won't close. b. It's out of gas. c. It's making a funny sound.
4. "Is the gas tank full?"
   a. No. That's it. b. Oh, no! I forgot to fill it up. c. I wasn't paying attention.

LESSON 3

11 **Read the ads for the three cars. Then choose the best answer to each question, according to the ads. Circle the letter.**

RAMUNO

The Ramuno is really inexpensive, and you'll find it easier than ever to own one today. You can start saving money because it's good on gas. You can even save time parking when you drive a Ramuno—with the Ramuno's size, you'll never have to worry if you can only find a tight parking spot.

RAMUNO

Love outdoor adventures? Feel the power of the four-wheel drive Vicic. It'll take you just about anywhere. The new design allows you to enjoy a comfortable ride even on the toughest mountain roads. Come test-drive it today!

Zatec

You'll be amazed by how the Zatec provides comfortable seating for nine people and still has plenty of cargo room. Whether it's a few suitcases for your family's road trip or all the bags from a long day's shopping at the mall, you won't have any problem fitting them all in.

1. Which of the three cars can take the most passengers?
   a. the Vicic b. the Zatec c. the Ramuno
2. What type of car do you think the Zatec is?
   a. a sports car b. a full-size sedan c. a van
3. Which of the three cars is most likely a compact car?
   a. the Ramuno b. the Vicic c. the Zatec

12 **Read about the people. Which of the three cars in Exercise 11 is best for each person? Explain your reasons.**

1. Bryan is planning a cross-country road trip with his girlfriend. They want to do a lot of sightseeing in the countryside and go hiking in the mountains.

   ____

   ____

2. Rachel has four kids and she works part-time. She has a lot of driving to do for work, the kids, and shopping. And she needs to carry a lot of things around.

   ____

   ____

3. Danny recently graduated from college and has just started working. He doesn't have a lot of money. He's single and lives by himself. His office is on a busy street downtown, far away from where he lives. He plans to drive to work.

   ____

   ____

13 Extra reading comprehension

Read *Six Tips For Defensive Driving* on page 46 of the Student's Book again. Then read the statements and write D for defensive driving, A for aggressive driving, or I for inattentive driving.

1. _____ tailgating to make others go faster
2. _____ following the "3-second rule"
3. _____ multitasking while driving
4. _____ checking your mirrors frequently
5. _____ slowing down in bad weather
6. _____ pulling over to avoid a bad driver
7. _____ cutting other drivers off
8. _____ talking on the phone while driving

14 **Read the article about renting a car in the U.S.**

Driving in the U.S.A.

Planning a trip to the U.S.? Have you thought about how you'll get around? If you're going to stay in a big city such as New York, Chicago, or San Francisco, public transportation is the most convenient option. However, to travel almost anywhere else in the U.S., you'll need a car.

Car Rental Tips

Requirements: Most car rental agencies require drivers to be at least 25 years old. Some allow younger drivers but may charge a higher rate. To rent a car in the U.S., you will need a credit card and driver's license. Visitors can usually rent a car and drive with a driver's license from their home country. However, if your license is in a language that doesn't use the Roman alphabet, you should obtain an International Driving Permit in English.

Cost: Car rental rates change often, and you can usually save money by shopping around for the best price. Be sure to check travel and rental agency websites for special sales and discounts. Look for package deals that offer car rental and airfare or hotel for one low price. If your schedule is flexible, compare prices for different travel dates. It is often cheaper to rent a car on weekends or for a full week rather than a few days.

Hidden charges: Always read the small print on your car rental agreement carefully—to check for hidden charges such as taxes, airport surcharges, and drop-off fees (an extra charge for returning a car to a different location from where you picked up). Make sure that you drop off the car with a full tank of gas. Rental agencies charge a fill-up fee and high gas prices if they have to fill up the gas tank.

Safety: Before you leave the car rental lot, inspect the car carefully for damage and make sure everything is working properly. Ask the agent to note any problems on the rental form. Take a few minutes to become familiar with the car. Adjust your seat and mirrors. Locate the controls for the lights, turn signals, and windshield wipers. Then, buckle up! Wear your seat belt, and ask your passengers to wear theirs, too. Most states have seat belt laws, and all states require that young children and babies sit in the back seat in special child seats. When you're ready, follow the traffic laws for the states you'll be driving in. If you're not sure, check with car rental staff before you hit the road.

SOURCES: usatourist.com, novacarhire.com

15 **Find and circle the phrases in the article in Exercise 14. Then match the phrases and their meanings. Write the letter on the line.**

1. _____ get around
2. _____ package deals
3. _____ hidden charges
4. _____ fill-up fee
5. _____ buckle up
6. _____ hit the road

a. extra costs that are not clearly stated
b. fasten your seat belt
c. travel from place to place
d. begin a car trip
e. specials that offer two or more services for one price
f. an extra charge for returning a car without a full tank of gas

16 **Answer the questions about renting a car in the U.S. Use information from the article in Exercise 14. Explain your answers.**

1. I am 23 years old. Can I rent a car? ______________________________

____

2. Do I need an International Driving Permit to drive in the U.S.? ______________________________

____

3. Where can I get the best price for a car rental? ______________________________

____

4. I want to pick up a car in New York and drop it off at Los Angeles International Airport. What hidden charges should I check for? ______________________________

____

5. We are traveling with small children. Are there any special requirements? ______________________________

____

GRAMMAR BOOSTER

A **Complete each sentence in your own way. Use the past continuous or the simple past tense.**

1. They were having dinner when ______________________________.
2. While ______________________________, it started to rain.
3. While Marie was watching TV, her husband ______________________________.
4. When ______________________________, I was leaving my office.
5. He had an accident while ______________________________.

B **CHALLENGE. Look at the pictures. On a separate sheet of paper, write a story about what happened using the words and phrases in the boxes.**

drive talk on cell phone not pay attention	run in front of stop	hit hurt damage

C **Put the words in order and write sentences. If a sentence can be written in two ways, write it both ways.**

1. dropped / Margo / off / the car
   Margo dropped off the car. OR Margo dropped the car off.
2. up / it / Sam / picked
   ____
3. the tank / filled / I / up
   ____
4. can't / turn / on / Sue / the headlights
   ____
5. turn / off / I / can't / them
   ____
6. like / He'd / it / to / drop / off / at noon
   ____
7. I / to / need / up / it / fill
   ____
8. picked / the car / William / up / has
   ____

D **Label each underlined noun either <u>common</u> or <u>proper</u>. Then rewrite each sentence, replacing the underlined noun with a subject or object pronoun.**

1. common
   <u>The car door</u> is making a funny sound.
   It is making a funny sound.
2. <u>Mr. Lee</u> rented the convertible.
   ____
3. The mechanic replaced <u>the taillight</u>.
   ____
4. Alex already called <u>Econo-Car</u>.
   ____
5. <u>The Amigo minivan</u> hit the tree.
   ____
6. My sister will drop off <u>the keys</u>.
   ____
7. Mrs. Lane is going to pick up <u>her son</u> at 5:00.
   ____

WRITING BOOSTER

A **Insert commas where necessary in the following sentences.**

1. You need a driver's license and a credit card to rent a car.
2. The car rental charge included a drop-off fee a fill-up fee and an airport surcharge.
3. You should shop around for the best price and make a reservation.
4. Adjust your seat mirrors and the radio.
5. Locate the controls for the lights and turn signals.

B **Combine each pair of sentences into one sentence consisting of two independent clauses. Use <u>and</u>.**

1. The driver wasn't paying attention. He hit the car in front of him.

   ____

2. It's raining. The sunroof won't close.

   ____

3. Lucy has five kids. She drives a minivan.

   ____

4. The GPS isn't working. We're lost.

   ____

C **Complete the statements. Look back at the article in Exercise 14 for ideas. Add commas.**

1. Many areas of the U.S. don't have good public transportation. Therefore ______________

   ____.

2. Car rental rates change frequently. Therefore ______________________

   ____.

3. To find a good rate, check travel and car rental agency websites. In addition ______________

   ____.

4. Return your rental car with a full tank of gas. If you don't, you'll pay double the regular price for gas. In addition ______________________________

   ____.

5. Most states have seat belt laws. Therefore ______________________

   ____.

6. Small children must sit in the back seat. In addition ______________________

   ____.

D **On a separate sheet of paper, write about your driving or a friend or family member's driving. Include good and bad driving behaviors.**

UNIT 5

Personal Care and Appearance

Preview

1 **Complete the sentences with salon services.**

1. Your fingernails look great. Did you get a _ _ (_) _ _ _ _ _?
2. His hair was getting long, so he made an appointment for a _ (_) _ _ _ _ _.
3. I have a lot of tension in my shoulders from sitting at the computer. I need a _ _ _ (_) _ _ _.
4. After my _ _ _ _ _ (_), my skin felt smooth and soft.
5. I don't need a _ _ _ _ _ (_) _. I just washed my hair.

Now unscramble the circled letters. What's the word? ____________

2 **Complete the conversation with questions from the box. Write the letter.**

a. Do you think I could get a massage, too?
b. Is it customary to leave a tip?
c. How long will I have to wait?
d. Would it be possible to get a facial?
e. Can I charge it to my room?

Client: _____ (1.)? I don't have an appointment.

Receptionist: You're in luck. A client just canceled his appointment.

Client: Great. _____ (2.)?

Receptionist: Yes. But you might have to wait a bit.

Client: _____ (3.)?

Receptionist: Let's see. I have something at 4:00.

Client: That's fine. _____ (4.)?

Receptionist: Certainly. Just sign here, please. Then I'll show you to the dressing area.

Client: I have one more question. _____ (5.)?

Receptionist: That's up to you. But most clients give about 10 percent.

3 **How often do you get these salon services? Look at each picture and write a sentence.**

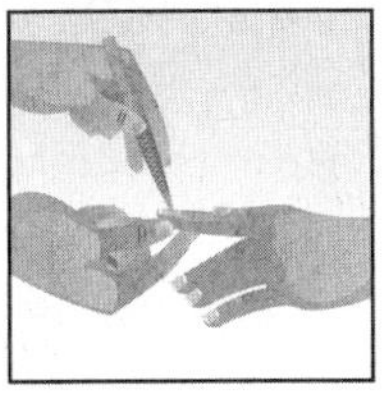
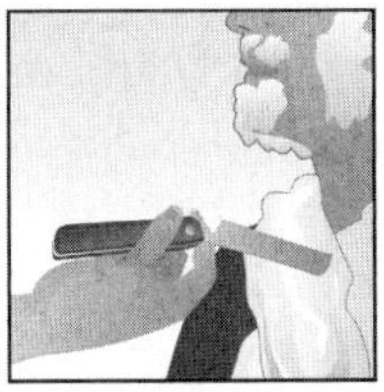
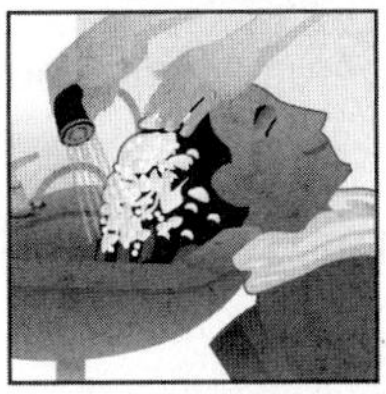
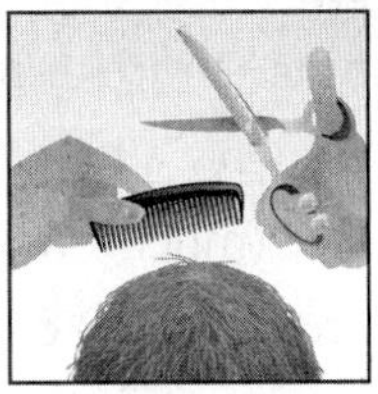
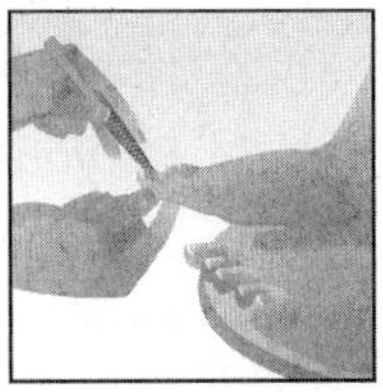

1. ______________________________
2. ______________________________
3. ______________________________
4. ______________________________
5. ______________________________

LESSON 1

4 **Complete the word webs. Write personal care products on the lines.**

1. Tooth care
2. Nail care
3. Hair care
4. Skin care
5. Shaving
6. Makeup

5 Complete the sentences. Circle the correct words.

1. This store doesn't have (much / many) combs.
2. I can't find (some / any) sunscreen, but here's (some / any) body lotion.
3. Do you have (much / a lot of) razors at home?
4. She doesn't have (much / many) hair spray left.
5. Emma needs (some / any) dental floss.
6. Helen doesn't need (some / much) soap.
7. Do you have (any / many) deodorant?
8. I have (some / any) extra shampoo.
9. I found shaving cream, but there aren't (some / any) razors here.
10. Are you out of toothpaste? I have (some / much).

LESSON 2

6 Complete each statement or question with <u>someone</u>, <u>no one</u>, or <u>anyone</u>. In some cases, more than one answer is correct.

1. ______________ made a ten o'clock appointment for a pedicure.
2. Excuse me. ______________ is at the front desk. Can ______________ help me?
3. I'm sorry. We don't have ______________ available to help you now.
4. There's ______________ ahead of you. Do you mind waiting?
5. Did you see ______________ you know at the hair salon?
6. There's ______________ waiting for a massage.

7 Look at the pictures. Write statements using the words in parentheses and <u>someone</u>, <u>no one</u>, or <u>anyone</u>. In some cases, more than one answer is correct.

1. (get / shave) *There's someone getting a shave.*
2. (give / facial) ______________
3. (get / haircut) ______________
4. (use / comb) ______________
5. (give / massage) ______________
6. (use / shampoo) ______________
7. (get / manicure / pedicure) ______________
8. (use / nail file) ______________

8 Extra reading comprehension

Read the article *Cosmetic surgery—for everyone?* on page 56 of the Student's Book again. Then match the terms with their definitions.

1. _____ chocoholic
2. _____ liposuction
3. _____ hair restoration
4. _____ depilatory
5. _____ face-lift
6. _____ chemical peel

a. a cream that removes unwanted hair on the body
b. surgery to correct baldness
c. someone who likes chocolate very much and eats it all the time
d. surgery to remove wrinkles and other signs of aging from the face
e. treatment for wrinkles that removes the top layer of skin on the face
f. surgery to remove fat from the body

9 **Read the article about ways to improve personal appearance.**

Look Great — Without Cosmetic Surgery

Want to lose weight? Look younger? More and more people are turning to cosmetic surgery. While liposuction or a face-lift might sound like an easy way to get the results you want, it's important to remember that cosmetic surgery is, in fact, surgery. And surgery is not easy. It's expensive, painful, and potentially dangerous. So, before you go under the knife, give these safe, low-cost ways to improve your appearance a try.

1. Get enough sleep. It's called "beauty sleep" for a reason. Nighttime is when your skin and hair cells renew and repair themselves. Also, more blood flows to your skin when you're sleeping, making it brighter. Most people know that lack of sleep can cause dark circles under your eyes. But many don't realize that not getting eight hours of sleep a night can also lead to wrinkles and weight gain.

2. Drink a lot of water. Get into the habit of drinking more water. Well-hydrated skin is less likely to develop blemishes or wrinkles. For clearer, smoother skin, try to drink at least eight glasses of water a day. The more water you drink, the better your skin will look. Also, drinking water throughout the day will curb your appetite—making it easier to eat less and lose weight.

3. Exercise regularly. The physical benefits of exercise include reduced body fat and more toned muscles. While 60 minutes of daily vigorous exercise is ideal, begin with a reasonable goal—maybe 30 minutes three times a week. Choose something you enjoy, and enroll in a class, join a team, or make plans to workout regularly with a group of friends.

4. Eat a healthy diet. To lose weight, you need to change your eating habits. You should choose foods that are low in fat and low in calories. You probably knew that already, but did you know that some foods can also improve the appearance of your skin and hair? For beautiful skin, eat foods rich in antioxidants. Darkly colored fruits and vegetables contain antioxidants, which help repair sun damage and prevent wrinkles. Blueberries, spinach, and carrots have a lot of antioxidants. For shiny, healthy hair, eat foods high in lean protein like fish, beans, and nuts. These foods may also help prevent hair loss.

What's good for your health is also good for your looks. So, get a good night's sleep and some exercise. Drink lots of water and eat fresh, natural foods—mostly fruits and veggies. It costs almost nothing and doesn't hurt, so what have you got to lose? Except maybe a few kilos!

Source: ehow.com

10 Complete the chart. Use information from the article in Exercise 9. How much sleep, water, and exercise does the article recommend? What types of foods does it suggest?

	What the article recommends
sleep	
water	
exercise	
diet	

11 What are the results of doing what the article recommends?

sleep —

water —

exercise —

diet —

12 CHALLENGE. How much sleep and exercise do you get? How much water do you drink? What types of foods do you eat? After reading the article, what would you like to do differently? Why?

13 **Think of a famous person or someone you know that represents both inner and outer beauty. Describe the person's inner qualities on the lines inside the head. Describe the person's physical features on the lines outside the head.**

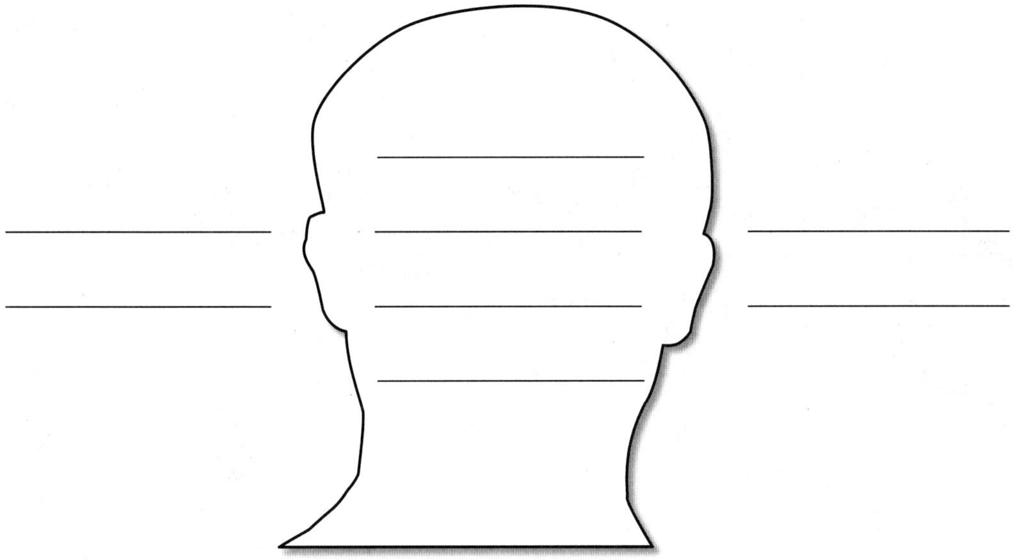

Name of person: ____________________

14 **Complete the statements with words from the box.**

attractive	health	heart	inner
kindness	modest	outer	patient

1. Someone who is a good listener and lets others speak is ____________.
2. Beautiful skin and hair and a nice body are features of ____________ beauty.
3. Goodness, ____________ to other people, truthfulness, and happiness with life are qualities of ____________ beauty.
4. Someone who has nice physical features is ____________.
5. The condition of a person's body is called ____________.
6. Someone who doesn't talk proudly about his or her own appearance or abilities is ____________.
7. "The best and most beautiful things in the world cannot be seen, nor touched . . . but are felt in the ____________." –Helen Keller

GRAMMAR BOOSTER

A **Look in the medicine cabinet. Write sentences about the products you see, using words from the box.**

bar	bottle	can	package	tube

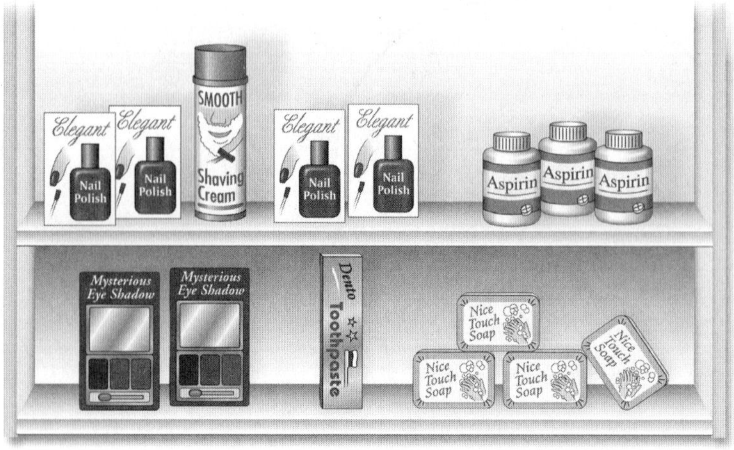

1. There are four bottles of nail polish.
2. ______
3. ______
4. ______
5. ______
6. ______

B **Answer the questions about your own personal care products. Write complete sentences with some or any.**

1. Do you have any dental floss at home?

   ______

2. Do you need some toothpaste from the store?

   ______

3. Is there any shaving cream in your bathroom?

   ______

4. Are you wearing any perfume or aftershave now?

   ______

5. Do you have some sunscreen at home?

   ______

6. Is there any makeup in your bathroom?

   ______

7. Would you like some hand lotion?

   ______

C Write a ✓ next to the sentences that are correct.

1. ☐ **a.** There isn't enough soap.
   ☐ **b.** There isn't too many soap.
2. ☐ **a.** Do you have too much razors?
   ☐ **b.** Do you have too many razors?
3. ☐ **a.** I don't have too many makeup.
   ☐ **b.** I don't have enough makeup.
4. ☐ **a.** Does she have too many toothpaste?
   ☐ **b.** Does she have enough toothpaste?
5. ☐ **a.** There isn't too much shampoo.
   ☐ **b.** There isn't too many shampoo.

D Complete each sentence with too much, too many, or enough.

1. I couldn't wash my hair. There wasn't ________________ shampoo left.
2. I'm going to the store. Do you have ________________ flour to make the cake?
3. There are just ________________ people here. I don't feel like waiting.
4. Don't you think that's ________________ money for a pedicure? It's too expensive.
5. You bought ________________ nail files. We only need one.

E Complete each sentence with fewer or less.

1. Bridget should wear ____________ makeup. She looks beautiful without it!
2. Budget hotels have ____________ amenities than expensive hotels.
3. This film has ____________ violence than that new action adventure movie.
4. The compact car will use ____________ gas than the SUV.
5. Which ticket line has ____________ people waiting in it?
6. The rental agency has ____________ cars with manual transmission than with automatic transmission.

F Complete each sentence with something or anything.

1. We have ________________ new at our salon.
2. He didn't take ________________ for his headache.
3. Do you need ________________ from the drugstore?
4. I didn't see ________________ I like in the catalog.
5. I always buy ________________ from that store.
6. I just can't relax. There is always ________________ to do.
7. They gave me ________________ to drink at the salon.
8. I don't know ________________ about cosmetic surgery.

G **Read the paragraph. Find and correct five mistakes.**

> I went to the supermarket today because I needed to get nothing to cook for my dinner party tonight. I wanted to buy some juice, too. But when I got there, there wasn't nothing on the shelf! I went to the store manager and asked him why the shelves were empty.
> He apologized and said there was anything wrong with the delivery truck. "It didn't come today," he told me. He said I'd have to wait until the next day. Now I don't have something to serve for the big party tonight. I've never seen nothing like this!

WRITING BOOSTER

A **Think about a time when you had bad service at a place of business such as a salon, a car rental agency, a hotel, a movie theater, or a restaurant. Write an e-mail message to the manager complaining about the service. Describe the problem you had. Suggest a way for the business to improve.**

To:	
Subject:	

B **Prepare to turn your e-mail message into a formal business letter. Write the following information.**

1. your address: ______
2. recipient's name and / or position and address:
   ______
3. today's date: ______
4. a salutation: ______
5. a complimentary close: ______
6. your signature and printed name: ______

C **Now type (or write) your formal business letter. Use the e-mail message you wrote in Exercise A as the body of your letter. Include all the information from Exercise B.**

About the Authors

Joan Saslow

Joan Saslow has taught in a variety of programs in South America and the United States. She is author of a number of multi-level integrated-skills courses for adults and young adults: *Ready to Go: Language, Lifeskills, and Civics; Workplace Plus: Living and Working in English;* and of *Literacy Plus.* She is also author of *English in Context: Reading Comprehension for Science and Technology.* Ms. Saslow was the series director of *True Colors* and *True Voices.* She participates in the English Language Specialist Program in the U.S. Department of State's Bureau of Educational and Cultural Affairs.

Allen Ascher

Allen Ascher has been a teacher and a teacher trainer in China and the United States and taught in the TESOL Certificate Program at the New School in New York. He was also academic director of the International English Language Institute at Hunter College. Mr. Ascher is author of the "Teaching Speaking" module of *Teacher Development Interactive,* an online multimedia teacher-training program, and of *Think about Editing: A Grammar Editing Guide for ESL.*

Both Ms. Saslow and Mr. Ascher are frequent and popular speakers at professional conferences and international gatherings of EFL and ESL teachers.

Authors' Acknowledgments

The authors are indebted to these reviewers who provided extensive and detailed feedback and suggestions for the second edition of *Top Notch* as well as the hundreds of teachers who participated in surveys and focus groups.

Manuel Aguilar Díaz, El Cultural Trujillo, Peru • **Manal Al Jordi,** Expression Training Company, Kuwait • **José Luis Ames Portocarrero,** El Cultural Arequipa, Peru • **Vanessa de Andrade,** CCBEU Inter Americano, Curitiba, Brazil • **Rossana Aragón Castro,** ICPNA Cusco, Peru • **Jennifer Ballesteros,** Universidad del Valle de México, Campus Tlalpan, Mexico City, Mexico • **Brad Bawtinheimer,** PROULEX, Guadalajara, Mexico • **Carolina Bermeo,** Universidad Central, Bogotá, Colombia • **Zulma Buitrago,** Universidad Pedagógica Nacional, Bogotá, Colombia • **Fabiola R. Cabello,** Idiomas Católica, Lima, Peru • **Emma Campo Collante,** Universidad Central Bogotá, Colombia • **Viviane de Cássia Santos Carlini,** Spectrum Line, Pouso Alegre, Brazil • **Fanny Castelo,** ICPNA Cusco, Peru • **José Luis Castro Moreno,** Universidad de León, Mexico • **Mei Chia-Hong,** Southern Taiwan University (STUT), Taiwan • **Guven Ciftci,** Faith University, Turkey • **Freddy Correa Montenegro,** Centro Colombo Americano, Cali, Colombia • **Alicia Craman de Carmand,** Idiomas Católica, Lima, Peru • **Jesús G. Díaz Osío,** Florida National College, Miami, USA • **Ruth Domínguez,** Universidad Central Bogotá, Colombia • **Roxana Echave,** El Cultural Arequipa, Peru • **Angélica Escobar Chávez,** Universidad de León, Mexico • **John Fieldeldy,** College of Engineering, Nihon University, Aizuwakamatsu-shi, Japan • **Herlinda Flores,** Centro de Idiomas Universidad Veracruzana, Mexico • **Claudia Franco,** Universidad Pedagógica Nacional, Colombia • **Andrea Fredricks,** Embassy CES, San Francisco, USA • **Chen-Chen Fu,** National Kaoshiung First Science Technology University, Taiwan • **María Irma Gallegos Peláez,** Universidad del Valle de México, Mexico City, Mexico • **Carolina García Carbajal,** El Cultural Arequipa, Peru • **Claudia Gavancho Terrazas,** ICPNA Cusco, Peru • **Adriana Gómez,** Centro Colombo Americano, Bogotá, Colombia • **Raphaël Goossens,** ICPNA Cusco, Peru • **Carlo Granados,** Universidad Central, Bogotá, Colombia • **Ralph Grayson,** Idiomas Católica, Lima, Peru • **Murat Gultekin,** Fatih University, Turkey • **Monika Hennessey,** ICPNA Chiclayo, Peru • **Lidia Hernández Medina,** Universidad del Valle de México, Mexico City, Mexico • **Jesse Huang,** National Central University, Taiwan • **Eric Charles Jones,** Seoul University of Technology, South Korea • **Jun-Chen Kuo,** Tajen University, Taiwan • **Susan Krieger,** Embassy CES, San Francisco, USA • **Robert Labelle,** Centre for Training and Development, Dawson College, Canada • **Erin Lemaistre,** Chung-Ang University, South Korea • **Eleanor S. Leu,** Soochow University, Taiwan • **Yihui Li (Stella Li),** Fooyin University, Taiwan • **Chin-Fan Lin,** Shih Hsin University, Taiwan • **Linda Lin,** Tatung Institute of Technology, Taiwan • **Kristen Lindblom,** Embassy CES, San Francisco, USA • **Ricardo López,** PROULEX, Guadalajara, Mexico • **Neil Macleod,** Kansai Gaidai University, Osaka, Japan • **Robyn McMurray,** Pusan National University, South Korea • **Paula Medina,** London Language Institute, Canada • **María Teresa Meléndez de Elorreaga,** ICPNA Chiclayo, Peru • **Sandra Cecilia Mora Espejo,** Universidad del Valle de México, Campus Tlalpan, Mexico City, Mexico • **Ricardo Nausa,** Centro Colombo Americano, Bogotá, Colombia • **Tim Newfields,** Tokyo University Faculty of Economics, Tokyo, Japan • **Mónica Nomberto,** ICPNA Chiclayo, Peru • **Scarlett Ostojic,** Idiomas Católica, Lima, Peru • **Ana Cristina Ochoa,** CCBEU Inter Americano, Curitiba, Brazil • **Doralba Pérez,** Universidad Pedagógica Nacional, Bogotá, Colombia • **David Perez Montalvo,** ICPNA Cusco, Peru • **Wahrena Elizabeth Pfeister,** University of Suwon, South Korea • **Wayne Allen Pfeister,** University of Suwon, South Korea • **Cecilia Ponce de León,** ICPNA Cusco, Peru • **Andrea Rebonato,** CCBEU Inter Americano, Curitiba, Brazil • **Elizabeth Rodríguez López,** El Cultural Trujillo, Peru • **Olga Rodríguez Romero,** El Cultural Trujillo, Peru • **Timothy Samuelson,** BridgeEnglish, Denver, USA • **Enrique Sánchez Guzmán,** PROULEX, Guadalajara, Mexico • **Letícia Santos,** ICBEU Ibiá, Brazil • **Lyndsay Shaeffer,** Embassy CES, San Francisco, USA • **John Eric Sherman,** Hong Ik University, South Korea • **João Vitor Soares,** NACC, São Paulo, Brazil • **Elena Sudakova,** English Language Center, Kiev, Ukraine • **Richard Swingle,** Kansai Gaidai College, Osaka, Japan • **Sandrine Ting,** St. John's University, Taiwan • **Shu-Ping Tsai,** Fooyin University, Taiwan • **José Luis Urbina Hurtado,** Universidad de León, Mexico • **Monica Urteaga,** Idiomas Católica, Lima, Peru • **Juan Carlos Villafuerte,** ICPNA Cusco, Peru • **Dr. Wen-hsien Yang,** National Kaohsiung Hospitality College, Kaohsiung, Taiwan • **Holger Zamora,** ICPNA Cusco, Peru.